The Truth about Jesus

The challenge of evidence

Paul Barnett

AQUILA

A book by Aquila Press

Published July 1994. Reprinted 1997, 2000
Copyright © Paul Barnett

Scripture taken from the
HOLY BIBLE, NEW INTERNATIONAL VERSION
Copyright © 1973, 1978, 1984
by International Bible Society

Aquila Press
PO Box A287, Sydney South, NSW Australia 1235

National Library of Australia
ISBN 1 875861 02 5

For John Chapman

About the Author

Paul Barnett was educated at Manly Boys' and Gosford High Schools. He then worked as a cadet quantity surveyor, attending evening classes at the University of Technology for five years to qualify as a Quantity Surveyor. He was converted to Christianity in his final year of study. After qualifying he worked as a Quantity Surveyor for a number of years before entering Moore Theological College in 1960. In 1963 he was ordained and commenced full-time ministry.

Paul Barnett holds the Licentiate in Theology and Scholar in Theology awards from the Australian College of Theology, Bachelor of Divinity degree from the University of London, Master of Arts from the University of Sydney and a Doctor of Philosophy from the University of London.

He has held ministry positions as rector of St Barnabas' Broadway (1967–1973) and of Holy Trinity Adelaide (1973–1979). Appointed Master of Robert Menzies College in 1980, he was co-founder and Senior Minister of University Church, Macquarie University. In 1990 he became Bishop of North Sydney.

Bishop Barnett has had a 30-year association as a lecturer with Moore Theological College and has also lectured at the Adelaide Bible Institute. He has a long association with the divinity courses at the University of Sydney, the History Department at Macquarie University, the School of Christian Studies which he founded in 1983, and, since 1987, Regent College Vancouver, where he was appointed as a Distinguished Visiting Scholar.

Paul Barnett has written regularly for the media and made many radio and television appearances.

Six books have been published since 1986: *Is the New Testament History?* (1986); *The Message of 2 Corinthians* (1988); *Bethlehem to Patmos* (1989); *Apocalypse Now and Then* (1989); *The Two Faces of Jesus* (1990); and *The Servant King* (1991). A major commentary on 2 Corinthians is near completion.

i

Forewords

E.A. Judge
Emeritus Professor of History, and Director Ancient History Documentary Research Centre, Macquarie University

An ancient historian has no problem seeing the phenomenon of Jesus as an historical one. His many surprising aspects only help anchor him in history. Myth or legend would have created a more predictable figure. The writings that sprang up about Jesus also reveal to us a movement of thought and an experience of life so unusual that something much more substantial than the imagination is needed to explain it.

On the one hand the New Testament texts are intimately at home in their world (even showing us sides of it rarely seen in other sources). Yet on the other they embody some radically different ideas and assumptions about it. This raises tantalising questions for the historian. Any careful reader is also confronted by personal issues not easy to cope with.

Those who cannot enter into the perspective of the New Testament writers may be driven to rationalisation of what happened. Such gambits (often dramatised in the media) may be so speculative or fantastic that people lose sight of the elementary and commonsense character of the historical data.

Dr Paul Barnett is an experienced historian, trained in a hard school. He has a keen eye for bare facts. He understands the distinctive character of different New Testament writings. The grouping of them into four parallel sets each documenting successive stages of the tradition about Jesus explains how their differences help identify the 'core facts'. The observation of 'gratuitous' (or incidental) testimony reinforces this.

I have cleared my head while reading this book in ways that were new to me. I recommend it to those who want a quick but up-to-date re-assessment of the historical truth about Jesus.

✳   ✳   ✳

Keith Mason QC
Solicitor General for New South Wales

Every legal contest (civil or criminal) involves the interaction of three matters: (1) the (true) facts as they occurred in the past; (2) the evidence or means whereby the judge or jury gets a window through which to search for the facts; and (3) a verdict, which represents a decision about the impact of the facts as found.

So too with much of life. In both great and small matters we are constantly confronted with these three aspects of decision-making. For example, my decision about where to go on holidays this year may be based on how I recall and perceive the actuality of last year's holiday. There is nothing unusual about this exercise. Only the human ostrich avoids it in the contemplation of the larger issues of life's purpose and death significance.

The concept of evidence is central to every endeavour, not just the lawyer's. Though the rules differ from field to field, what they have in common is a consensus about what works according to human experience.

Paul Barnett invites us all, believers, unbelievers and doubters, to journey with him on a truth-seeking mission. In the words of a famous American judge we are to approach with an 'open mind, not an empty one'. We are to test the evidence of those apostles who spoke and wrote conscious of their role as 'witnesses'. The processes Barnett adopts are very familiar to a lawyer: the presentation and testing of evidence; the search for corroboration from external sources; the comparison of overlapping accounts to see if they can be substantially reconciled without such identity of form and substance as to show contrived collaboration; and the search for that 'ring of truth' that comes from loose ends and rough edges. The lawyer is also most familiar with the means of testing the credibility of witnesses that are used in this work. Did the witnesses have sufficient opportunity to observe? Do their actions conform to their words? Is there independent support for their account, and how weighty is it? What motive did they have to lie or to tell the truth?

On the last topic, it is pertinent to remember that the Greek word for witness is the one from which we derive the English word 'martyr'. The most compelling witnesses to the life, work, teaching, death and resurrection of Jesus Christ were those who were to die as martyrs. Amongst the key martyrs of the early Church were those whose credibility as historical witnesses is examined closely by Dr Barnett: Paul, Peter and James.

The legal process is designed to move from doubt and controversy to decision. Even if the decision is to acquit because the accused is given the 'benefit of the doubt', lawyers wrestle sceptically with the evidence and welcome challenge and testing as the best means of approaching the truth. But there is always a purpose – to arrive at a verdict (literally, a true saying). This purpose is fundamental to this challenging book.

Contents

Chapter One

Inquirers into Jesus

At 12.30 p.m., 22 November 1963, John F. Kennedy, President of the United States of America, was shot in his car en route to a civic reception in Dallas, Texas. Those old enough to remember will never forget the impact on them of the news flashes: 'President Kennedy is dead!' Almost as dramatic as the death of the charismatic young president was the shooting, two days later and televised live, of the arrested Lee Harvey Oswald in the Dallas City Jail at the hands of Jack Ruby.

Questions immediately arose. Who was really responsible for the president's assassination? Was there one marksman or two? Did Lee Harvey Oswald act on his own account or was he the instrument of a sinister conspiracy against the president?

Answers to these questions touch the national interest of all Americans. Such answers, if they could be found, would only be arrived at by careful inquiry.

At 3.00 p.m. Friday, 3 April AD 33, the young rabbi Jesus, from Nazareth, died by crucifixion at the hands of Roman executioners outside the walls of Jerusalem.[1] As from the Sunday following, and for the next forty days, he was seen alive on at least twelve occasions, by between 500 and 600 people. The truth about what happened to John F. Kennedy matters deeply to the American people. The truth about

---

1   The date has been established by scientists C. Humphreys and W.G. Waddington
     Nature 306, 1983, 743–746. According to Mark 15:34 Jesus died at the 'ninth hour'
     (3.00 p.m.).

1

what happened to Jesus of Nazareth matters profoundly to all people everywhere. His death, it is claimed, is for God's forgiveness of our sins; his resurrection, for the destruction of the power death holds over us. Everybody has a stake in the truth about who Jesus was and what really happened to him.

INQUIRY INTO GOD

When the Bible states that 'the Word became flesh and lived for a while among us'[2] it is saying that the One who was responsible for the creation of the universe and of time *himself came into that universe at a particular time*. In other words, it declares that in Jesus of Nazareth God entered human history, leaving his footprints for us to discover.

Inquiry into Jesus, therefore, is *historical* inquiry. How does one pursue this inquiry? Inquiry into the claims about Jesus, like the questions about John F. Kennedy, begins by reflecting on historical information. After a period one comes to a conclusion, and a 'position' is adopted. But at the beginning the focus is on those historical footprints of Jesus and, in this regard, inquiry into Jesus is exactly the same as for any other person or event within history: by an examination of the evidence for and about Jesus in the period in which he lived.

This is not to say that John F. Kennedy and Jesus of Nazareth are of equal importance. Jesus is – it is asserted – the Saviour of the world; John F. Kennedy was merely a president of one of the nations of the world. In recent times, however, questions have been raised about the basic truth of Christianity.

Contemporary doubts: Thiering and Spong

It may be thought that scholars like Barbara Thiering and

---

2   John 1:14.

2

John Shelby Spong, with the cooperation of the popular media, have so effectively discredited previously held views of Jesus that further inquiry into Jesus is unnecessary.

According to Dr Thiering, Jesus was crucified by the Dead Sea, not at Jerusalem, was drugged and did not die, subsequently revived, later married and then divorced Mary Magdalene, only to remarry another woman and then die in old age.[3]

Dr Thiering finds the key to understanding Jesus in the Dead Sea Scrolls, initially discovered at Qumran in 1947. She identifies John the Baptist and Jesus with two shadowy persons who appear within the Scrolls: John the Baptist is the Teacher of Righteousness and Jesus is the Wicked Priest.

But there are two fatal objections to this theory. One is that, according to almost all scholars, these Scrolls belong to an earlier period of Jewish history, pre-dating John and Jesus by nearly two hundred years. The Wicked Priest is thought to be one or other of the Maccabean rulers of the second century BC and the Teacher of Righteousness a devout teacher who led his followers out of corrupt mainstream society to establish the true people of God. The second objection is that the few references in the Scrolls to the Teacher and the Priest establish no linkages with John the Baptist or Jesus. In other words, Dr Thiering has done nothing more than create a historical fantasy, which, ironically, many people believe just because it is so fantastic.

Professor A. D. Crown, an eminent Jewish scholar who is an acknowledged authority on the Scrolls, dismisses Dr Thiering's work as 'fiction...and sand castles' and as having 'an outrageous chronology and some very strange explanations'.[4] Another reviewer observes: 'This is not really a book about the Dead Sea Scrolls. It is a fantastical reinterpretation of the gospels and the life of Jesus

---

3   B. Thiering, *Jesus the Man* (New York, Doubleday, 1992).
4   *Annals,* June, 1992, 14–15.

supposedly using a technique unlocked by the scrolls.'[5]

Bishop Spong writes that Jesus was not born of a virgin – rather, that Mary the mother of Jesus had been sexually violated. He asserts that the marriage at Cana, recorded in the second chapter of the Gospel of John, was actually between Jesus and Mary Magdalene. Moreover, Bishop Spong does not believe that Jesus was raised bodily from the dead. There was no tomb, hence there could be no empty tomb: Jesus' corpse was thrown into a common grave. The resurrection occurred in the spirit of Peter six months after the event; Jesus' whole life and death had been the sign of God's love.[6]

Spong's works are quite speculative at many points. For example, there is not the slightest evidence for his propositions that Mary was sexually violated or that Jesus married Mary Magdalene at Cana; both conclusions are entirely conjectural. He approaches the Gospels with the presupposition that supernatural events – miracles – do not occur.

Spong proceeds to dismantle the evidence of the New Testament about Jesus' virgin conception and physical resurrection in two ways. First he looks for arguments to support his presupposition about miracles, by authoritatively declaring what would or would not have actually happened in that culture, as with marriage customs of the day. But the reality is that our knowledge of the culture remains incomplete. Many pieces of the jigsaw are missing, in all probability lost forever. A certain tentativeness must be observed by true scholars, especially when reconstructing ancient cultures.

Then he heaps up apparent historical contradictions within the Gospels, particularly in relation to the accounts of

5   *Biblical Archaeological Review* Sept/Oct, 1992.
6   J.S. Spong, *Born of a Woman: A Bishop Re-Thinks the Birth of Jesus* (San Francisco, Harper, 1992); *Resurrection: Myth or Reality* (San Francisco, Harper Collins, 1994).

4

Jesus' resurrection appearances. Again, at this distance, it is risky to assert dogmatically that the texts are contradictory. If we had more information and a fuller picture some present difficulties would surely disappear. In any case, historical discrepancies among the sources do not of themselves disprove the event thus reported. Josephus gives varying accounts of the details of Herod Antipas' banishment by Caligula in AD 39: the *Jewish War* states that Antipas was banished to Spain, whereas in the *Antiquities of the Jews* he is banished to Gaul.[7] Despite the contradiction, there is no doubt that he was banished from his tetrarchy of Galilee–Peraea. Writers of antiquity, including the writers of the New Testament, did not have at their disposal sophisticated maps, calendars or library resources, nor were footnotes yet invented! It would not be until the recent centuries that historians would seek the precisions we now expect. If the Gospel accounts agreed in every last detail we might well suspect that a conspiracy had occurred. The loose ends imply the probability of integrity.

A noted scholar of Christian origins, Dr N.T. Wright, comments that Bishop Spong 'gives an amazingly caricatured picture of church history to sustain his rhetoric' and that 'he gives rein to pure fantasy which...puts him outside the bracket of serious scholarship'.[8] Despite glimpses of scholarship at some points, Bishop Spong's reconstructions are essentially conjectural.

Between them Dr Thiering and Bishop Spong have cast serious doubt on the critical sequence in the Christian Creed about Jesus – that he was 'born of the virgin Mary', that he 'suffered [crucifixion] under Pontius Pilate' and that 'the third day he rose again from the dead'. Thanks to Thiering and Spong, who purport to be dispassionate scholars, many people may now think that the things taught about Jesus in

---

7   *Jewish War* ii.181-183; *Antiquities of the Jews* xviii.252.
8   N. T. Wright, *Who was Jesus?* (London, SPCK, 1992). In this book, Wright analyses the writings of Dr Thiering, Bishop Spong and A. N. Wilson.

traditional Christianity have been exposed as untrue.

Thiering and Spong, who are both best-selling authors, have enjoyed popular acclaim for their radical assault on Christian belief. But neither author has been supported by the body of reputable scholars – Jewish, Christian or agnostic.

Multiculturalism

At the same time as Christianity has been subject to these intellectual attacks a cultural revolution has been occurring in many countries. Former 'Christian' societies like those of Britain and Europe have become 'multicultural'. High levels of immigration by peoples from Muslim, Buddhist and Hindu countries have changed the cultural mix. Alongside the cross on the church steeple may now be seen the crescent on the minaret of the Muslim mosque. The peoples to whom churches have been sending missionaries are now living in great numbers as equal members of the same communities, with their religions afforded the same place in public broadcasting and school curricula which a decade or so ago was the sole preserve of the churches.

Moreover, in countries like the United States of America, Canada and Australia there is now deep awareness and appreciation of the culture that prevailed prior to European settlement. Many feel considerable sympathy for those aboriginal peoples and the spirituality of their cultures, with accompanying hostility towards that 'Christian' culture which violently imposed itself on the indigenous peoples and their religions. Those ancient aboriginal religious cultures are seen to be entirely agreeable with various powerful and popular movements of our times such as feminism, new age mysticism and environmentalism.

It would not be surprising if many who were nominally Christian are now thinking that Christianity has no more claim to truth than, for example, Islam or Hinduism or the religion of indigenous Australians.

6

So is Christianity true? Can a person of integrity become, or for that matter remain, a Christian?

HISTORY, NOT MYTH

It is fundamental that we understand Christianity to be based in historical reality. Jesus was a true figure of history, who ministered as a rabbi and prophet in Judaea during the prefecture of Pontius Pilate under whom he was executed by crucifixion on the Friday before Passover. No less historical is his physical resurrection, which occurred sometime on Saturday night so that his burial tomb was found to be empty by early Sunday morning.

The Christian religion is constructed upon these historical facts. To disprove these facts would be to destroy the essential character of Christianity. This has always been the situation, though there are many who wish to see Christianity as merely a matter of 'experience' based on the nobility of Jesus' sacrifice and of his love.

Indeed, from the very beginning of its history, the attempt has been made to portray Christianity as a matter of inner 'illumination', as a kind of mystic experience. With its grossness and clamour, human existence in the world was regarded as evil, something from which to escape into the eternal calm of heaven above in the presence of God. Thus the process of finding God was by way of abstinence from the things of this world, especially eating and sexual intercourse, accompanied by deep and mystical meditation. One climbed a spiritual ladder, progressively purifying oneself, to merge one's soul with the soul of God in heaven.

This view of 'salvation' was widespread in the world culture into which the apostles of Christ came preaching his Gospel. Fundamental to 'Gnosticism', as this movement is called with its claim to superior 'mystical-knowledge', is the insistence that matter is evil; only God above is good and pure. Thus, for the Gnostic, Jesus only 'appeared' to be truly man. No incarnation, that is, God coming in the *flesh*,

7

could be possible. Moreover, a *bodily* resurrection would be quite impossible. The 'story' of Jesus' incarnation and resurrection are redemptive *ideas,* rungs to climb to redemption out of this earthly mess. But they must not be historically true. They remain 'myth', concepts that are experientially helpful, but which did not and could not happen. For the Gnostic, incarnation and resurrection are both 'bodily', part of the historical fabric, itself evil, from which one must be redeemed.

In their desire to 'contextualise' and so spread the Gospel more easily in that culture, it would have been very easy, and indeed appealing, for the apostles to adapt their message to the 'gnostic', non-material, non-historical view. It is striking, however, that the apostles are implacably opposed to this option at every turn. Let me give some examples:

Speaking of Jesus' life, the apostle *John* states that '[the life] which was from the beginning, which we have heard, which we have seen with our eyes, which we have looked at and our hands have touched...appeared'.[9] This person Jesus was real. He 'appeared' to a group for whom John speaks, who 'heard', 'saw' with their own eyes and physically 'touched' him. He became physically a part of history, open to inquiry and investigation.

Luke is deeply aware of the historical character of Jesus. Near the beginning of his Gospel he refers to John the Baptist, who announced the arrival of the long-awaited One. In a remarkably precise historical statement Luke notes: 'In the fifteenth year of the reign of Tiberius Caesar − when Pontius Pilate was governor of Judaea, Herod tetrarch of Galilee, his brother Philip tetrarch of Iturea and Traconitis, and Lysanias tetrarch of Abilene − during the high priesthood of Annas and Caiaphas, the word of God came to John'.[10] The Messiah-announcing ministry of John is pinpointed to a precise year of Tiberius' rule of the Roman

---

9 1 John 1:1-2.
10 Luke 3:1-2.

Empire (AD 28), cross-referenced by the verifiable incumbencies in four neighbouring principalities, with the overlapping military and ecclesiastical headships respectively of Pilate and Annas/Caiaphas in Judaea. This is the language of history, which would be abhorrent to the Gnostic's mythical–mystical outlook.

Peter tells his readers that 'when we – apostles – made known to you the power and coming of our Lord Jesus Christ we did not follow sophisticated myths but we became *eyewitnesses* of his majesty'.[11] Peter immediately gives as an example the occasion when Christ was transfigured on the mountain. Peter and his companions were present with Jesus on that mountain where they *'heard'* the voice of God from heaven, and Peter emphasises 'we were *with* him'. They were at the place at that time and they saw and heard what happened. He assures his readers that in teaching them about Jesus Christ, he has neither followed nor devised 'myths'; his information is *historical* in character. Humanly speaking, there was nothing to be gained by taking this line; the letter is written against those who are coming under Gnostic influence.

Paul knew that in Corinth there were those who rejected the idea of the future resurrection of their bodies. In correcting their misunderstanding, Paul reminds them that the message which they originally received, and by which they became Christians, was grounded in the bodily resurrection of Jesus. He repeats what he had originally told them, namely that, according to the Gospel, Christ died, was buried, was raised on the third day and appeared on six separate occasions to many hundreds of witnesses. How can they reject the idea of bodily resurrection when their very standing as Christians rests in the bodily resurrection of Jesus?[12] What emerges unintentionally and without design

---

11 2 Peter 1:16 (my translation).
12 1 Corinthians 15:1-19.

from Paul's words is the factual nature of Christ, the 'that-ness' of the Gospel about him. That Christ really died is confirmed by the statement that he was buried. That he rose bodily, as opposed to 'rising', in some ghostly or imaginary manner, is confirmed by the detail that it occurred 'on the third day' and, moreover, that so many saw him alive on so many different occasions.

By what they have written John, Luke, Peter and Paul reveal that the Jesus they proclaim – his coming, his death, his resurrection – is historical, that he really did come, that his death by crucifixion in Jerusalem actually took place and that he physically reappeared three days later alive from the dead.

EVIDENCE AND EXPERIENCE

The author of this book did not set out in life as a Christian. It was only in my final year at University that I acknowledged Jesus to be Lord in my life. I was overwhelmed to discover that God loved me and that his Son had died for me. The mysteries of life – why is the world the way it is, who am I and why am I here – began to make sense. For me the point of entry was a matter of 'experience'.

But was Christianity *factually* true? To the 'experiential' and 'existential' there would need to be added the *evidential*. I undertook university studies in Ancient History and Greek to evaluate the strength of the evidence for Jesus.

While many are moved, as I was, to become Christians because of the 'existential', sooner or later the 'evidential' must also be confirmed. That, certainly, was my personal experience. Conversely, there are some who will not begin to expose themselves to the *existential* until they have resolved the *evidential* questions. They will not expose themselves to a religious commitment until they are sure of the facts. Indeed, the existential and the evidential are the twin pillars on which Christian faith rests.

Thus this book is written for two groups of readers:

It is for those who are already Christians and who need answers to the truth questions about Jesus. Because of the steady assault on Jesus and the Gospels through newspapers, magazines and television many people think Christianity has now been discredited factually. Some, indeed, may be at the point of giving up the faith or may even have done so.

But it is also for those who are not yet Christians, but who are open to becoming Christians once those truth questions about Jesus are resolved. You are attracted by Jesus, his teaching and the forgiveness and strength he offers, but you are not sure that these are based in reality. This book will help you deal with your doubts and uncertainties.

Is a relationship with Jesus, then, limited to inquiry into a figure of history? Not at all. Whenever personal commitment to Jesus is entered into, the very Spirit of God comes into our lives, binding our inner beings to God as our Father and Jesus as our Lord. The moral personality of Jesus is imparted to us and begins to be expressed in our own behaviour. To pray to God our Father, to live under the Lordship of Jesus, to read the Scriptures as the Word of God, to meet with other believers in praise of God are profoundly real experiences. This experience of God arises as a result of personal commitment, which in turn follows our decision concerning the truth about Jesus Christ.

ASSUMPTIONS

The author should declare his assumptions about the status of the Bible. I regard the Bible as the Word of God, God's own 'breath' or Spirit, which we encounter in the written Scriptures. This is a view which many do not hold. But please do not stop reading. The inquiry that I wish to undertake in the following pages does not depend on my belief that the Bible is the Word of God.

11

Rather, this investigation into the truth about Jesus depends on another significant assumption, which I ask you to share with me: that the books of the New Testament are genuine historical documents, valid sources of information, on a par with non-Christian writers of the time like Josephus and Tacitus. It is this reasonable assumption which I ask you to accept in examining the truth about Jesus from the evidence of history.[13]

QUESTIONS FOR REFLECTION AND DISCUSSION:

1. Why are evidence and truth important for Christians and Christianity?

2. Discuss the contemporary perceptions of Christianity which see it as outmoded or irrelevant.

3. Why is inquiry into Jesus more important than knowing the cause of John F. Kennedy's death?

4. Gnosticism was part of the cultural background of the New Testament. What are the parallels to Gnosticism today and how do they bear on Christianity?

FURTHER READING:

P.W. Barnett, *Is The New Testament History?* (Sydney, Hodder & Stoughton, 1986).

N.T. Wright, *Who was Jesus?* (London, SPCK, 1992).

---

13 The reader is referred to my books *Is The New Testament History?* (1986), *Bethlehem to Patmos – The New Testament Story* (1990), and *The Two Faces of Jesus* (1986), each published by Hodder & Stoughton, Sydney.

Chapter Two

Truth about Jesus' existence

People often ask if there is evidence for Jesus, apart from within the New Testament. In this chapter we will investigate evidence for Jesus in non-Christian writings, as well as references to the Jesus-movement. We will also consider 'dovetailing' references from inside and outside the New Testament to people and places.

EVIDENCE IN NON-CHRISTIAN WRITINGS

Overwhelmingly, it is true, the evidence for Jesus comes from his followers, and is recorded in the New Testament. But there is also some information about him from others, including those who stood outside the Christian community, some of whom were relatively neutral, others of whom were quite hostile.

Direct references to Jesus

Josephus, an aristocratic Jew, born AD 37 and raised in Jerusalem, could not fail to have been aware of 'the Nazarene sect', as the early Christians were called by their critics.[1] He wrote:

> About this time there lived Jesus, a wise man, if indeed one ought to call him a man. For he was one who wrought

---

1   Acts 24:5.

surprising feats and was a teacher of such people who accept
the truth gladly. He won over many Jews and many of the
Greeks. He was the Messiah. When Pilate, upon hearing him
accused by men of the highest standing amongst us, had
condemned him to be crucified, those who had in the first
place come to love him did not give up their affection for
him. On the third day he appeared to them restored to life,
for the prophets of God had prophesied these and countless
other marvellous things about him. And the tribe of
Christians, so called after him, has still to this day not
disappeared.[2]

Although Josephus' brief note about Jesus is controversial,[3] it does have an authentic historical ring at a number
of points: (1) Josephus states that Jesus was a 'wise man...a
teacher', that is, a sage or devout rabbi, who worked
miracles. The Gospels corroborate this view of Jesus.
Nicodemus, an eminent Jew of the period, addressed Jesus
as 'Rabbi...a teacher...[who performs] signs'.[4] (2) This Jesus
achieved considerable popularity; he 'won over' both Jews
and Greeks, that is, Hellenistic or Greek-speaking Jews. We
know of Hellenistic Jews within Israel at that time from both
the Gospels and the Acts of the Apostles.[5] (3) In what
sounds like opinion reported to him, Josephus records that
Jesus was 'accused by men of the highest standing among
us', that is, among Josephus' fellow aristocrats, a group to

2   Josephus, *Antiquities of the Jews* xviii.63.
3   While many scholars doubt that Josephus would use 'faith' language about Jesus,
    suggesting that Christians have subsequently made additions to the text, few reject it
    outright. At the very least even the most sceptical see a core of authentic information
    about Jesus. The passage is to be found in all original manuscripts and in earliest
    external citation of it (Eusebius, *History of the Church* i.11). A tenth-century Arabic version
    of Josephus' passage recorded by Agapius, Bishop of Hierapolis, omits 'if one ought to
    call [Jesus] a man' and while stating that 'he was perhaps the Messiah', nonetheless
    asserts that 'his disciples...reported that he had appeared to them three days after his
    crucifixion, and that he was alive'. Agapius' passage may be close to Josephus' original
    words.
4   John 3:2.
5   John 12:20; Acts 6:1,5,9.

whose opinions Josephus had access. (4) Roman trial procedure is implied by 'Pilate, hearing him accused...condemned him to be crucified'. Accusation followed by condemnation is precisely what happened in the Gospel accounts. (5) 'On the third day Jesus appeared to *them*' — that is, the Jews and Greeks he had previously 'won' — 'restored to life'. Notice Josephus' distinction between *us* aristocratic Jews and *them*, that is, the Christians. Peter indicates that *only to his followers* did Jesus show himself when raised from the dead.[6]

Information about Jesus probably came to Josephus during his boyhood, that is, within two decades of the historical Jesus, although he did not write it down until the nineties in Rome. Reflecting on the continued existence of followers of Jesus he commented: 'the tribe of Christians, so called after [Jesus], has still to this day not disappeared'.

Josephus is no Christian. His statements 'if one ought to call [Jesus] a man' and that 'he was the Messiah',[7] whose restoration to them alive was according to what 'the prophets of God had prophesied' should not be taken as Josephus' own convictions, but rather as reflecting his understanding of the views of Christians towards Jesus. On the other hand, Josephus is not hostile to Jesus. His lack of hostility, in contrast with that displayed towards various revolutionary and partisan prophets of the time, is probably due to Josephus' perception that, unlike those persons, Jesus was apolitical, a non-agitator. Although the final text of Josephus is debated, the evidence is there that Jesus was a teacher and miracle worker who influenced many Jews from Palestine and abroad; that he was thought by his followers

---

6   Acts 10:41. Nonetheless, Jesus also appeared to those who were not his followers at the time, for example the unbelieving brother James and the persecutor Saul of Tarsus.

7   The Christian scholar Origen, writing in the third century, specifically declared that Josephus did 'not believe in Jesus as the Christ' (*Against Celsus* i.xlvii; cf. *Commentary on Matthew* on 10:17). Origen may simply be reflecting the known fact that Josephus was not a Christian. Later in the *Antiquities* Josephus writes of Jesus as the 'so-called Messiah' (xx.200).

to be the Messiah, and that he was executed by the Roman governor Pontius Pilate at the instigation of the Jewish religious authorities.

Tacitus, our other main non-Christian source, is hostile. The greatest of the Roman historians of the period, Tacitus describes the great fire of AD 64 which destroyed the greater part of the city of Rome and for which the Emperor Nero himself had been blamed by the people. Tacitus, a boy of seven when the fire began, was, at the time of writing his *Annals of Imperial Rome,* the governor of the province of Asia (western Turkey). Nero commissioned an extensive rebuilding programme in the years immediately following the fire. Neither this, nor the sacrifices to the gods, erased the widely held suspicion that Nero was directly or indirectly responsible for the fire.

Emperor Nero

According to Tacitus, Nero sought to divert attention from himself by fastening the blame on 'the notoriously depraved Christians, as they are popularly called'. Tacitus' careful detail about Christus, their 'originator', probably reflects an actual official report from Judaea, rather than popular Roman gossip about Christus and Christians. Tacitus wrote:

> Christus, from whom the name [Christians] had its origin, suffered the extreme penalty during the reign of Tiberius at the hands of one of our procurators, Pontius Pilatus, [in] Judaea...[8]

Although Christus is here the malefactor's name, it is also consistent with the accusation against him noted in the Gospels, namely that he was 'the Christ'. The official charge – 'the king of the Jews' – was attached to the execution cross[9] and to a Roman governor would have approximated to the Jewish term the 'Messiah' or 'the Christ'. Doubtless Tacitus knew the extreme penalty meant crucifixion. It is unmentioned because cultivated Romans would not bring themselves to refer to that grossest form of punishment reserved to suppress the lower orders. Tacitus is precise in other details: the criminal met his just deserts in Judaea, during the governorship of Pontius Pilate (AD 26–36). Because Pilate was so obscure, Tacitus must indicate that the Emperor in whose epoch these events took place was Tiberius (AD 14–37).

How did the followers of Christus come to be in Rome? Tacitus proceeds to mention how this disease-like movement spread to the world-capital:

> ...the deadly superstition, thus checked for the moment, broke out afresh in Judaea, the first source of the evil, but

---

8   *Annals of Imperial Rome* xv.44.
9   John 19:19.

also in the City, where all things hideous and shameful from every part of the world meet and become popular…[10]

Revolutionary movements in Palestine generally died with the deaths of their leaders. Tacitus doesn't explain why this 'deadly superstition' was not stopped in its tracks by the execution of Christus, its originator, but *broke out afresh*. The apostles would have no difficulty accounting for this: God raised Christus from the dead!

For his part Tacitus, the conservative Roman, fears this movement as a 'deadly superstition', an 'evil' and something 'hideous and shameful'. The apostles, however, say that it is by the power of the newly given Spirit of God that the good news crossed the seas to be received by so many at the heart of the empire. Although their interpretations of the founder and his movement are utterly opposed, Tacitus and the apostles are entirely agreed as to the naked facts: Christ was executed in Judaea at the hands of Pontius Pilate and his movement did not stop but spread to Rome. This information must be regarded as historically secure.

A reign of terror, extending over many months (c. AD 65–66), now fell upon the Christians of Rome. Tacitus, no friend of this sect, was sickened by the extremes of cruelty against them perpetrated by Nero.

Less certain references to Jesus

Alongside Josephus and Tacitus are other references to Jesus from outside the New Testament. These, however, either due to lateness or indirectness, are to a degree problematic, and of secondary value.

Phlegon was a Greek historian of the second century whose writings are known through the quotations of others;[11] his own works have not survived. *Origen,* the third-

---

10   *Annals of Imperial Rome,* xv.44.
11   Origen, as quoted following, but also Julius Africanus, *Extant Writings* xviii.

century Christian apologist, appeals to Phlegon in his defence of the Gospel accounts in a number of areas: (1) Against the charge that Jesus was in fact incapable of predicting the future, Origen cites Phlegon who had indicated that Jesus prophesied future events which had been fulfilled.[12] It is likely that these related to Jesus' prophecies about the destruction of the Temple, which was fulfilled in AD 70. (2) In support of the darkness and the earthquake at the time of the crucifixion Origen notes that Phlegon indicates that such things did indeed occur in the time of the Emperor Tiberius.[13] (3) In one place Origen quotes directly from Phlegon that 'Jesus, while alive was of no assistance to himself, but that he arose after death, and exhibited the marks of his punishment, and showed how his hands had been pierced by nails'.[14] From this it appears that Phlegon knew of the circumstances of Jesus' death and resurrection, very probably from the Gospels.[15]

Based on this indirect and slender data it appears that, at the least, Phlegon is aware of the last part of the Gospel story — the prophecies on the Mount of Olives, Jesus' helplessness at the time of his arrest, the darkness and the earthquake at the time of the crucifixion, and the bodily nature of the resurrection. Origen's use of Phlegon supports the case for the authenticity of his record.

The first century Samaritan chronographer, *Thallus,* in the third book of his *History,* mentions a time of total darkness caused by a solar eclipse occurring in Palestine at this time. The Christian chronographer, *Julius Africanus,* while noting Thallus' information, attributes the darkness to God's direct action.[16]

The *Rabbi Eliezer,* who is thought to belong to the period

---

12 Origen, *Against Celsus,* ii.xiv.
13 Origen, *Against Celsus,* ii, xxxiii, lix.
14 Origen, *Against Celsus,* ii, lix.
15 Luke 24:40; John 20:20.
16 Julius Africanus, *Extant Writings,* xviii. Thallus' own work has been lost.

between AD 70–200, appears to be referring to Jesus, though he does not mention him by name. Rabbi Eliezer offers a slanted interpretation of an ancient oracle of Balaam, which in its original had ascribed truthfulness to God ('God is not a man, that he should lie...').[17] In Eliezer's hands Balaam's words are infused with prophetic power against an unnamed man:

> Balaam looked forth and saw that there was a man born of a woman who should rise up and seek to make himself God, and cause the whole world to go astray. Therefore God gave power to the voice of Balaam that all the peoples of the world might hear, and thus he spake, 'Give heed that you go not astray after that man; for it is written, God is not a man that he should lie. And if he says he is God he is a liar, and he will deceive and say that he departeth and cometh again at the end. He saith and he shall not perform.'[18]

Who is this man who says firstly, that he is God and secondly, that he will come again at the end? Surely the Rabbi is using Balaam's ancient words in a modern setting to portray Jesus as this liar, who, mere man that he was, taught that he was God, and, moreover, that he would come back at the end. Evidently Jesus was being accorded a considerable following at that time. Eliezer says that this liar had caused 'the whole world to go astray'.[19]

A Jewish tradition from the post-AD 70 period, and recorded in the *Talmud,* describes the fate of Jesus:

> Jesus was hanged on Passover Eve. Forty days previously the herald had cried, 'He is being led out for stoning, because he has practised sorcery and led Israel astray and enticed them

---

17   Numbers 23:19.
18   Quoted in J. Klausner, *Jesus of Nazareth* (London, Collier-Macmillan, 1929), 34.
19   On the original Palm Sunday the Pharisees, noting the great crowd attending Jesus said, 'The whole world has gone after him' (John 12:19).

82

to apostasy. Whosoever has anything to say in his defence, let him come forward and declare it.' As nothing was brought forward in his defence, he was hanged on Passover Eve.[20]

According to Jewish practice, a herald publicly announced accusations against a malefactor, providing opportunity for a defence to be offered. Jesus was accused of sorcery (his miracles?) and of leading Israel into error and apostasy (his distinctive teaching?). Since no defence was forthcoming Jesus was executed, not by stoning, but by 'hanging' (crucifixion?) on the Eve of the Passover.

Although the *interpretation* of Jesus is quite contrary to that offered by the apostles, the raw *facts* are in accord with the Gospels: Jesus was (1) a teacher and (2) a miracle worker who (3) was executed (4) at Passover time. Although the Gospels give no hint of a herald's public proclamation of his alleged crimes, it is by no means unlikely that such a process occurred. The Gospel of John presents Jesus embroiled in controversy in Jerusalem between the Feast of Tabernacles (October) and the Passover of execution (April), that is for about six months,[21] with some periods of withdrawal outside Jerusalem.[22] A forty-day public proclamation against him is consistent with this.

Inscriptions on ossuaries discovered in 1945 in Talpioth, a suburb of Jerusalem, are thought by Professor Sukenik to have been prayers directed to Jesus: 'Jesus save' and 'Jesus let him arise'. The fact that the ossuaries contained coins from just a few years after Jesus would offer intriguing evidence about belief in Jesus. Many scholars, however, are doubtful about the inscriptions, pointing to the uncertainty of the lettering.

The so-called *'Slavonic'* version of Josephus' *Jewish War*, which apparently dates from the eleventh century, but was

20 *Sanhedrin* 43a.
21 John 7 – 12.
22 John 10:40; 11:54.

An ossuary or bone chest

only published in 1906, contains a number of references to a 'wonder worker' not found in our Greek edition of Josephus' great work. Some scholars have argued that this old Russian version is a translation of Josephus' now lost Aramaic original, and that it is therefore more authentic than the Greek text on which our English translations are based.

How is Jesus presented in the 'Slavonic' Josephus? According to this version Jesus, who is not named, was 'a king who did not reign', a Moses figure come back to life who worked miracles but who broke the Sabbath. Although he resisted crowd pressure to lead an uprising against the Romans, for which he was charged before Pilate but acquitted by him, he was ultimately crucified by the Jews for prophesying the destruction of Jerusalem and the Temple.

The 'Slavonic' Josephus remains a mystery. Although most scholars dismiss its account of Jesus as garbled and unauthentic, certain questions remain unanswered. What motive could there be for a medieval scribe copying the seven lengthy volumes of Josephus' *Jewish War* to insert a number of short passages about Jesus? If that scribe was part of eleventh-century Slavonic culture, why is the Jesus of these passages merely a revived Moses who worked miracles and whom the crowds chose as a revolutionary leader? Why is this Jesus not the divine Son of God, the co-equal of the Father, whom we would find in the Greek and Russian Orthodox Church belief of that period? The obstinate resistance of these questions to satisfying answers leaves open the tantalising possibility that the 'Slavonic' Josephus records an authentic and primitive perspective of Jesus as he was viewed by sections of the Jewish community of that era, and which Josephus reproduced.

REFERENCES TO THE CHRISTIAN MOVEMENT

Pliny, the friend of Tacitus, draws attention to this movement. Tacitus and Pliny were governors of adjoining provinces at the same time, Tacitus in Asia, Pliny in Bithynia.

Whereas Tacitus writes about events fifty years earlier, Pliny's concerns are contemporary to the time of writing.[23] As one newly arrived in this Black Sea province, Pliny could not fail to notice the massive social and economic impact locally of the new movement, Christianity. On further inquiry into their activities, Pliny discovered that these Christians 'met regularly before dawn on a fixed day to chant verses alternately among themselves in honour of Christ as if to a god'. In his examination of them Pliny demanded those he had arrested to 'revile publicly the name of Christ', which he came to understand 'no genuine Christian can be induced to do'.

Two facts made this movement worrying to Romans like Tacitus and Pliny. Both writers note, first, the immense

---

23   *Epistles* x.96.

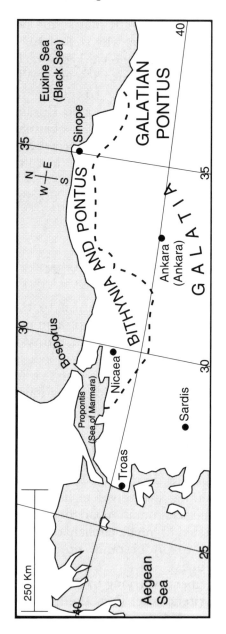
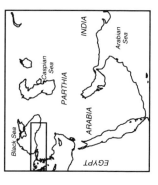

Map 1*: Bithynia*

24

popularity of the movement and, second, an implacable and
exclusive life-and-death devotion to someone other than the
Roman state and its Emperor. Only to Jesus, not to
Caesar/the Roman state, would these Christians direct their
worship. Technically, this made their activities a
'superstition', something private and exclusive in contrast
with state religion, which was public. In the eyes of Tacitus
and Pliny this movement was a serious threat to the social
order.

Suetonius, although writing a decade or two later than
Tacitus and Pliny, refers to events earlier than those
described by them. Suetonius briefly mentions a serious
eventuality in AD 49 when due to 'Chrestus' (probably a
spelling of 'Christus'),[24] the Emperor Claudius was forced to
expel the Jews of Rome from Italy.[25] Using rather similar
terms to Tacitus and Pliny, Suetonius speaks later of the
Christians as 'a class of men given to a new and wicked
superstition',[26] that is, a private and exclusive sect. So far as
Suetonius is concerned this movement is dangerously
disruptive to the good order of Roman society.

Benediction 12 is one of eighteen Benedictions formulated
by Jewish leaders in Jamnia in the years soon after the
disastrous war with Rome AD 66–70. This Benediction is
directed to 'the Nazarenes' and asks God that they 'perish'
and 'be blotted out from the book of life'.

Under the leadership of James, the brother of Jesus, many
Jews had embraced the faith of Jesus the Messiah in the
years leading up to the war. While these 'messianic' Jews
could live in relative harmony alongside their fellow-Jews
before the war, Benediction 12 makes clear that such Jews
were no longer welcome in the synagogues of Palestine.

---

24 Tertullian, the lawyer turned Christian, writing in the early third century, implies that
    Chrestus may have been a common variant of *Christus* (*Apology* 3:5). Indeed, in Codex
    Sinaiticus, the earliest manuscript of the whole New Testament, the three references to
    'Christian' (Acts 11:26; 26:28; 1 Peter 4:16) are spelled as 'Chrestian'.
25 *Life of Claudius* xxv.4; cf. Acts 18:12.
26 *Life of Nero* xvi.2.

What had made the difference? In all probability, it was their decision not to fight for Israel against the Romans, but to withdraw from Jerusalem to Pella in Transjordan, which polarised the Jewish community at large against the 'Nazarenes'.

Benediction 12 is clear evidence from a non-Christian outlook of the existence of this 'Jesus-movement' in the years after the great war AD 66–70. This evidence confirms the extensive record of Jewish Christianity in Israel in the half century after the Jewish revolt, as found in the Christian historian, *Eusebius*.[27]

In the following decades, Ben Kosiba, leader of the second Jewish revolt in Israel against Rome (AD 132–135), was regarded by many as Messiah. This is reflected in the name 'Bar Kochba' ('son of a star') by which he was popularly known. Ben Kosiba was intolerant of attention being accorded to any other messianic figure. According to Justin Martyr, a writer of that time, 'it was only Christians whom [he]…commanded to be punished…if they did not deny Jesus as the messiah of the Jews and blaspheme him'.[28]

Thus, with writers from Pliny to Eusebius there is clear evidence of the existence of the Christian movement, and significantly this evidence is from within a century of the historical Jesus.

THE 'DOVETAIL' FACTOR

The splayed tail of the dove gives its name to a series of splayed cuts used by cabinet makers and by which, for example, the sides of drawers are neatly fitted together. By careful cutting, joining and gluing the separate pieces are made into a perfect whole.

The inquirer into the truth about Jesus employs a similar

---

27 *History of the Church* iii.11-20.
28 Quoted in Eusebius, *History of the Church* iv.8.

process. Important information from two sides – the Christian and the non-Christian sources – dovetails together to form a coherent picture of Jesus within his immediate historical context. This information is about (1) people and (2) places and it is to be found in historical writers of the period as well as through the work of archaeologists.

People

In one passage from the Gospel of Mark and in one passage in Josephus we find references to two people who are important in the Jesus history. One is the prophet *John the Baptist,* the other is his murderer, the Jewish tetrarch *Herod Antipas,* known in both those sources simply as Herod.[29] John was the humble forerunner of Jesus the Messiah; Herod was the ruler of Galilee, where Jesus conducted so much of his ministry. The two passages dovetail significantly:

Mark[30]	Josephus
The whole Judaean countryside and all the people of Jerusalem went…to be baptized by **[John]** in the Jordan River.	Herod [Antipas] had put to death **John** surnamed the Baptist…who had exhorted the Jews…to join in baptism
Herod [Antipas] had bound **John** and put him in prison…because John [said] 'It is not lawful for you to have your brother's wife.'	**Herod** decided to strike first…before…his work led to an uprising. **John**…was brought in chains to Machaerus…

---

29 Herod Antipas must be distinguished from his father Herod (sometimes called 'the Great') and his half-nephew Herod Agrippa (cf. Acts 12:1).

30 Mark 1:5.

The king...sent...orders to   ...and there put to death.[32]
bring John's head...[31]

Both the Christian and the non-Christian sources corroborate the raw facts of the other – that John was a baptiser and popular teacher and that he was first arrested and then killed by Herod while in prison. At the same time each adds complementary data, on one hand that John's offence related to his criticism of Herod's marriage, and on the other that Herod feared John's popularity. Josephus tells us that John was imprisoned and killed in the fortress Machaerus whereas Mark explains that this occurred at the time of Herod's birthday celebrations. Herod's arrest of John in c. AD 29 signalled the beginning of Jesus' public ministry.[33]

Another example of dovetailing information is provided by *Pontius Pilate*'s trial and execution of Jesus in AD 33. Again the raw facts given by the Christian source and the non-Christian broadly corroborate each other:

Luke	**Tacitus**
[They] led...**[Jesus]** to **Pilate**...'We have found this man subverting our nation. He opposes payment of taxes to Caesar and claims to be **Christ,** a king.'[35]	[The Christians'] originator **Christ** had been executed in Tiberius' reign by the governor of Judaea, **Pontius Pilate.**[34]

If Tacitus gives us the broad picture of Pilate executing a political malefactor, Luke fills in the details of the charges which were made against him, namely, that he sought to

---

31   Mark 6:17, 27.
32   Josephus, *Antiquities of the Jews*, xviii.117 ff.
33   Mark 1:14; cf. John 3: 24.
34   *Annals* xv.44.
35   Luke 23:2.

subvert the nation by undermining Caesar's authority, while asserting his own.[36]

As it happens, Pilate is known to us from other sources. In 1961 an Italian archaeological team, working in Caesarea Maritima, the great seaport built by Herod, came across this inscription:

TIBERIEUM
PON]TIUS PILATUS
PRAE]FECTUS IUDA[EA]E

This precious artefact comes from the very time of Jesus. It dedicates to the Emperor Tiberius a building – a temple? – which has long since succumbed to the ravages of time. The one responsible for its construction was 'Pontius Pilatus' the 'Prefect of Judaea', the Roman magistrate who condemned Jesus of Nazareth to the cross.

Pilate is known from two other historical writers, apart from Tacitus mentioned above. Josephus describes the grave problems in Judaea arising from Pilate's attempt to 'overturn Jewish laws'. After ten years as prefect, he was recalled to Rome c. AD 37 to answer charges of the 'persecution' of numbers of the Samaritan people.[37] The other writer, the Jewish scholar Philo, wrote damningly of Pilate two or three years later that

> he was a man of inflexible disposition and very merciless as well as obstinate...his government [was marked by] acts of corruption...acts of insolence...his rapine...his habit of insulting people and his cruelty, and his continual murders of people untried and uncondemned and his never-ending and gratuitous and most grievous inhumanity.[38]

---

36 Jews regarded the Romans' demand that taxes be paid direct to the Roman Emperor as usurping God's prerogatives and as a reason to rebel against Rome. But Jesus had said that the taxes were to be paid (cf. Mark 12:13–17). The charges were emotive but false.
37 Josephus, *Antiquities of the Jews* xviii. 55 and 88.
38 *Embassy to Gaius* xxxviii.

Roman governors were notorious for their corruption and ruthless administration of the provinces. The remarks of Philo and Josephus, both of whom lived under Roman provincial government, suggest that the man under whom Jesus 'suffered' was of more than ordinary cruelty and severity. This is entirely consistent with scattered references in the Gospels which hint at his violent character. One such reference is Pilate's slaughter in Jerusalem of Galileans in the very act of sacrificing lambs for the Passover meal.[39] Another is the insurrection which occurred in Jerusalem some time before Jesus' final visit to the city, at which Barabbas and the insurgents crucified with Jesus were arrested.[40]

According to the Gospels, the high priest and president of the Sanhedrin (the sacred council of the Jews) at the time of Jesus' trial was *Caiaphas*.[41] Dovetailing with the Gospels, Josephus also mentions Caiaphas as high priest, adding his complete name, 'Joseph who was called Caiaphas'.[42] In August 1992, the Jerusalem Post reported the discovery of an ossuary in a cave in the Peace Forest on the outskirts of Jerusalem. This casket bears the name 'Joseph, Son of Caiaphas', almost certainly the high priest mentioned by the Gospels and Josephus. Here are three lines of evidence which converge, corroborating each other and helping complete the picture. The Gospels tell us Caiaphas was son-in-law of the patriarchal high priest Annas, Josephus gives us the name by which he was known – 'Joseph who was called Caiaphas' – and the ossuary the reason he was so called, namely, that he was 'Joseph, son of Caiaphas'.

---

39 Luke 13:1–3.
40 cf. Mark 15:7. Pilate's weakness in the face of the chief priests' pressure (John 19:12–16) probably reflects the fact that his patron and protector Sejanus had been removed from office as praetorian prefect and that Tiberius the Emperor, who had resumed the reins of power, was concerned to stop further assaults on his Jewish subjects in Rome and the provinces. Sejanus, who had been de facto emperor AD 26–31 and was known for his antipathy towards Jews, was now vulnerable in Judaea and quickly turned coward in the face of concerted resistance.
41 Matthew 26:3, 57; John 18:24, 28.
42 *Antiquities of the Jews* xviii.35; cf. xviii.95: 'Joseph surnamed Caiaphas'.

Thus the external sources – historians and the data from archaeology – support and at some points add to the Gospel picture of the political landscape of Jesus' times. Through this information we see on one side Herod Antipas removing the prophet John the Baptist, thus marking the beginning of Jesus' public ministry in Galilee. On the other side, we see Jesus' ministry in Judaea brought to its end at the Passover AD 33 through the combined actions of the high priest, Joseph son of Caiaphas, and the Roman prefect of Judaea, Pontius Pilate. While the extra-biblical and biblical sources sometimes disagree, overall they dovetail together, giving a coherent historical understanding of Jesus in his times.

Places

References to place are of fundamental importance in many court cases. Where was the scene of the crime? Can it be established whether the accused was present at that place at the time of the crime? Juries are very interested to know details of place. But so, too, are historians. Place is one of the specifics of historical analysis. While legal and historical process has become technical and sophisticated, the concern relating to place is by no means modern, but was fundamental also in the time of Jesus. Lawyers and historians of that era – whether in Jewish, Greek or Roman culture – understood the fundamental importance of *place* to truth questions.

Because they are self-consciously historical in character, the Gospels mention many places at which Jesus exercised his ministry. Such details about geography show that these documents are, indeed, historical in character.[43]

Those sceptical about Christianity understand the implications for truth about place. They pointed to the

---

43   See A.R. Millard, *Discoveries From the Time of Jesus* (Oxford, Lion, 1990); J. Finegan, *The Archeology of the New Testament* (Princeton, University Press, 1978).

Map 2: Israel in the time of Jesus' ministry

absence of any corroborating reference in history or archaeology to *Nazareth,* the village of Jesus' upbringing and the place which identified him as Jesus *of Nazareth.* If there was no such place as Nazareth at that time it meant that Jesus himself was called into question.

In 1962, however, inscriptions bearing the word Nazareth dated to c. AD 70 were discovered in Caesarea Maritima. Archaeological work in and around modern Nazareth has established the existence of a settlement there during the times of Jesus' ministry. The existence of Nazareth is not now in question.

Other places are well-established whether by reference in historical works of the period or by archaeology or both. *Bethlehem,* Jesus' birthplace, is mentioned in the Old Testament, the Jewish inter-testamental writings and in Josephus.

Jesus' baptism by John the Baptist occurred at '*Bethany* beyond the Jordan', that is, at or near a village on the eastern side of the Jordan River.[44] For the period until the arrest of John the ministries of the two men ran in parallel, Jesus' disciples baptising in the Jordan, but on the Judaean or western side,[45] and John at *Aenon* near Salim.[46] While no certain external cross-referencing to these places has appeared, John's precise 'Bethany *beyond the Jordan*' and 'Aenon *near Salim*' encourages confidence in his accuracy.

John's description of Jesus' ministry in *Samaria,* which, because of the Pharisees, he was forced to pass through on his return to Galilee from Judaea, is remarkably detailed. He came to the city of Sychar close to Joseph's field, Jacob's well and Mt Gerizim.[47] The well in the lower part of the Greek Orthodox Church on the outskirts of modern Nablus, opposite Mt Gerizim, is, in all probability, the exact place

---

44 John 1:28; 10:40; cf. 3:26. This is not the Bethany near Jerusalem (John 11:18).
45 John 3:22; 4:1–4.
46 John 3:23.
47 John 4:1–4,5,20.

where the conversation between a weary and thirsty Jesus and the Samaritan woman occurred at noon.[48]

Cana, near Nazareth, where Jesus attended a wedding, is spoken of by Josephus who used it as his military headquarters.[49] The Gospel of John is aware of its elevated location. Three times John mentions 'coming *down*' from Cana, which is located in the Galilean plateau, to Capernaum, which is at sea level on the shores of the Sea of Galilee.[50] Cana was on or close to the main trunk road which led to Capernaum.

The inland *Sea of Galilee* was at that time the centre of a fishing and fish-preserving industry, supporting the Gospels' picture of Jesus' first disciples as Galilean fishermen with frequent boat crossings of the sea. *Magdala,* a large town on the western shores of the Sea of Galilee and the home of Mary Magdalene, was known in the Talmud as 'Migdal of Fishes'. Josephus often speaks of it by a Greek name, Tarichaeae, which means 'salted fish'. In the drought of 1985, the lower than usual water level of the Sea of Galilee left exposed an eight-metre-long boat quite close to Magdala. This boat was in use, probably for fishing, in the time of Jesus.

Meanwhile, *Chorazin,* a town overlooking the northern part of the Sea, as well as the northern coastal towns of *Capernaum* and *Bethsaida* – in each of which Jesus was active[51] – have been the subject of ongoing archaeological investigation and reconstruction. The excavations at Capernaum yield a good picture of streets and houses in a town of Jesus' period.

The prominence of Jesus in *Galilee* and the attempt of the Galileans to hail him as Messiah[52] forced Jesus to operate

48 John 4:6–7.
49 *Life* 86.
50 John 4:47, 49, 51.
51 Jesus speaks of the unrepentant people of Chorazin, Bethsaida and Capernaum, towns where most of his miracles were performed (Matthew 11:20-24).
52 John 6:14–15.

outside the tetrarchy of the ever-watchful Herod Antipas. Antipas had already removed one popular prophet (John the Baptist); he would not hesitate to remove another. Thus the Gospel of Mark, in particular, describes the ministry of Jesus within the territories of the north-eastern city-states of *Tyre* and *Sidon,* in *Bethsaida* and *Caesarea Philippi* in the northern Tetrarchy of *Gaulanitis* and in the desert city-states of the *Decapolis.*[53]

The Gospel of John has a particular interest in Jesus' activities in *Judaea* and *Jerusalem.* In one of his visits to Jerusalem he describes a healing at *Bethzatha,* a pool with five porticoes, located near the Sheep Gate in the city wall.[54] Archaeologists have excavated a pool complex near the eastern wall of the Old City, within the monastery of St Anne, which they have identified as John's Bethzatha.

According to the Gospel of John, Jesus' final six months were mostly exercised in Jerusalem and Judaea. John punctuates Jesus' ministry by reference to three Jewish feasts, which he gives in the precise order in which they occur: (1) The feast of Tabernacles, which occurs in autumn.[55] (2) The Feast of Dedication in mid-winter, when, according to John, Jesus took shelter from the cold in the Portico of Solomon, which is known to been in a protected location.[56] (3) The Feast of Passover,[57] which fell in the spring.

During these final months John also mentions the *Pool of Siloam,*[58] located to the south of the Temple Mount, into which Hezekiah's Tunnel empties. The intrepid tourist can wade through Hezekiah's tunnel, emerging from the darkness into the Pool of Siloam, to which Jesus sent the blind man.

To escape from the dispute following that incident, Jesus

---

53 See Mark 6:45 – 9:32.
54 John 5:2.
55 John 7:2.
56 John 10:22–23; Josephus, *Jewish War* v.184-185; *Antiquities of the Jews* xv.401.
57 John 12:1.
58 John 9:11.

The Truth About Jesus

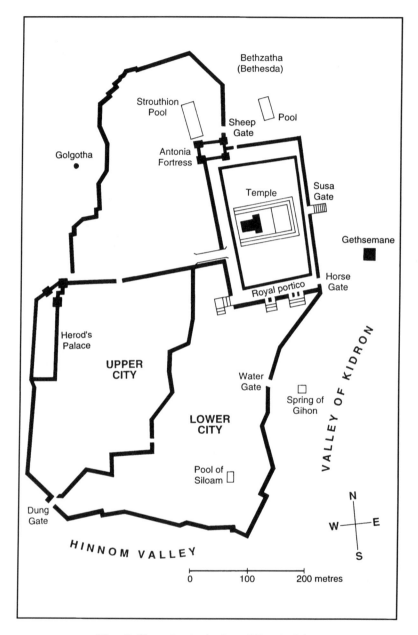

***Map 3**: Jerusalem in the time of Jesus' ministry*

36

withdrew to 'Bethany beyond the Jordan', as discussed above. From that Bethany he returned to '*Bethany*...about three kilometres from Jerusalem', on account of Lazarus' death. This Bethany is identified with the modern village El-Azariyeh, exactly three kilometres from Jerusalem on the road to Jericho. Eusebius, the fourth-century historian, who was familiar with Jerusalem, refers confidently to Lazarus' tomb. From that time, and probably earlier, this village has been called by a name derived from Lazarus.[59]

Once more forced to withdraw from Jerusalem, Jesus sought refuge in 'the country near the wilderness, to a town called *Ephraim*'.[60] While no town named Ephraim has been identified, the region of the tribe of Ephraim, hill country to the north of Jerusalem, is 'near the wilderness' of Judaea arising from the Jordan valley.

Like Matthew, Mark and Luke, John focuses the readers' attention on Jesus' final week, which was in *Jerusalem*. During this period many places in Jerusalem are mentioned – the large upper room, the Mount of Olives, the Kidron Valley, Gethsemane, the houses of Annas and Caiaphas, the Praetorium, Gabbatha and Golgotha. The thorough Roman destruction of the city in AD 70 and 135 and its subsequent rebuilding over earlier ruins have, to this point, not permitted sure identification of precise houses. Nonetheless, the sober manner of the narratives, the technical Roman 'Praetorium' and the vernacular Aramaic 'Gabbatha' and 'Golgotha' embedded in the Greek text, leave no doubt that specific places are being described. The excavation and restoration of palatial mansions from the Herodian period in the Jewish Quarter of the Old City give a vivid idea of the grand houses to which Jesus was taken on the night of his arrest.

What are we to make of the prominent religious sites in

59 Finegan, 91–92.
60 John 11:54.

Israel to which the modern-day tourist is taken? While many will find such churches commercialised and unedifying in the superstitious interest they arouse, it is likely that many of the actual locations are authentic. Although none of the present buildings pre-date the Crusader era of the Middle Ages, it seems that some, at least, were erected on sites of churches built in the fourth century when pilgrims began visiting the Holy Land. It is by no means unlikely that the first Christians knew of and noted the places where Jesus was known to have been born and put to death. A good case can be made for the authentic location of, for example, the Church of the Nativity in Bethlehem, the Church of All Nations (Gethsemane) in the Kidron Valley and the Church of the Holy Sepulchre. While the buildings and the uses to which they are put leave much to be desired, their erection may have preserved the position where events of historical significance regarding Jesus occurred.

Places are part of the data of inquiry, whether legal or historical. The examples given above indicate that the Gospels have numerous references to places significant in Jesus' ministry. Many of these places are able to be cross-checked in contemporary historical sources or archaeology or both. Such references to geography show that the Gospel records are historical, not mythological, in character.

What has an investigation of the external evidence for Jesus yielded?

Broadly speaking, these sources establish that Jesus was a genuine figure of history. It can be established that he lived and ministered in Galilee in the time of Herod Antipas; that he died in Judaea following the accusations of Caiaphas the high priest, by the hands of Pontius Pilate, the Roman governor; and that the movement led by him did not cease with his death, but continued and spread westwards to Rome. Numerous details about persons and places mentioned in the Gospels are corroborated, and at some points amplified, by external evidence. At no point do these details detract from or substantially contradict the Jesus we encounter in the pages of the Gospels.

The major difference is in the realm of interpretation as to the identity and mission of Jesus. The external sources, unlike the Gospels, do not attribute uniqueness or deity to Jesus. For these perpectives on Jesus we are entirely dependent on the New Testament.

QUESTIONS FOR REFLECTION AND DISCUSSION:

1. What do you make of the evidence for Jesus found in Josephus and Tacitus?

2. What are the implications of the dovetailing of people and places between the external sources and the Gospels?

3. Does this chapter impact on your sense of reality that Jesus was (or was not) a genuinely historical person? Do you feel it weakens or strengthens the historical reliability of the Gospels?

FURTHER READING:

P.W. Barnett, *Is The New Testament History?* (Sydney, Hodder & Stoughton, 1986).

P.W. Barnett, *Bethlehem to Patmos* (Sydney, Hodder & Stoughton, 1989).

F.F. Bruce, *The New Testament Documents: Are They Reliable?* (Leicester, IVP, 1979).

J. McRay, *Archaeology of the New Testament* (Grand Rapids, Baker, 1991).

D.Wenham, *Gospel Perspectives* Vol. 5 (Sheffield, JSOT, 1984).

Chapter Three

Truth about Jesus from Paul

According to popular and even scholarly opinion, Paul knew little about Jesus of Nazareth. Many think that Paul came decades later than Jesus and that he then perverted what Jesus had taught.

But this is simply not true. Even before his conversion Paul knew about Christ and Christians. He had heard them speak about Christ. Indeed, it was because he knew about them, and through them the Christ in whom they believed, that he persecuted them.[1] His own conversion from persecutor to believer occurred within a very brief space of time after the ministry of the historic Jesus.

When, as fellow-follower, not as oppressor, Paul came to know the leaders of the movement, more information was added to his previous knowledge of Jesus. Thus by the time his first Letters appear in AD 50 Paul knew a lot about Jesus Christ: as an early convert to Jesus Christ Paul had access to quality information about him, both before as well as after his own conversion.

His Letters, the earliest of which were written less than twenty years on from Jesus' crucifixion, make Paul a very early source of information about Jesus. Those Letters contain quotations from those who were believers before Paul, and include quotations from the Lord himself.

In the examination of Paul's evidence for Jesus in his Letters, those letters will be treated in this chapter as if they

---

1   Acts 26:9–11.

40

are ordinary documents of history rather than, as Christians believe, the inspired Word of God.

WHO WAS PAUL?

Paul was an approximate contemporary of Jesus. Unlike Jesus, however, Paul was not a Palestinian but a Diaspora Jew, that is, a Jew born outside the Holy Land. Originally known as Saul, he was born into a wealthy family of pure Jewish ancestry who were at that time domiciled in the Hellenistic university city of Tarsus in Cilicia (south-eastern Turkey). Paul's mother tongue, therefore, was Greek.

As a boy Saul was sent – or, if his parents re-settled in Jerusalem, brought – to Jerusalem to prepare for the rabbinate in the school of the distinguished Pharisee, Gamaliel.[2] To the Greek of the Diaspora, Paul now added the Hebrew of the Scriptures as well as the Aramaic of the man in the street. As a disciple of Gamaliel, the master-scribe, he acquired mastery of the Hebrew scriptures and of their legal interpretation.

By the time of Jesus' public ministry, Saul would have been a well-known figure in Jerusalem,[3] a teacher in his own right. The knowledge of the Greek version of the Old Testament reflected in his Letters, suggests that he had become a teacher in the Greek-speaking synagogues of Jerusalem, possibly for expatriate congregations like those from his own native Cilicia.[4] It is almost certain Paul was among those who unsuccessfully disputed with Stephen in such synagogues and who subsequently orchestrated the mob who seized Stephen and brought him to the Sanhedrin.[5]

Reflecting on his 'previous way of life in Judaism', Paul

---

2   Acts 22:3; 26:4.
3   Acts 26:4.
4   Acts 6:9.
5   Acts 6:10–13.

speaks of having been 'extremely zealous for the traditions
of my fathers', leading him to be 'advance[d] in Judaism
beyond many of my own age'. Such 'zeal' for the 'traditions'
of Israel also led him to 'persecute...violently the church of
God' and to attempt to 'destroy it'.[6]

This rising star among the Pharisaic zealots of Jerusalem
saw himself as the sword of the Lord, raised up to destroy
the blasphemous and heretical schism founded by the
crucified Nazarene, Jesus – a blasphemy which was
currently being proclaimed by Stephen and others who, like
Paul, were Greek-speaking Jews.

The Pre-Christian Paul Knew About Jesus

It is almost certain that Paul was in Jerusalem at the same
time as Jesus, and that he had heard him speak. His words
to the Corinthians, 'We knew Christ according to the flesh',[7]
appear to imply that.

It is quite certain that, within that first year or so after
Jesus, as we have suggested above, Paul had heard about
Jesus from preachers like Stephen. Certainly, Paul heard
Stephen's defence to the Sanhedrin of his faith in Jesus
which culminated in the accused's dying testimony to the
'Lord Jesus'.[8] After the stoning of Stephen, Paul immediately
led the assault on believers in the synagogues of Jerusalem.[9]
During these arrests and stonings Paul would have levelled
accusations at his victims and heard their testimonies to
Jesus.

There can be no doubt that the pre-Christian Paul knew
quite a lot about Jesus, though he was bitterly opposed to
him.

6   Galatians 1:13; Philippians 3:5–7; Acts 22:3–4.
7   2 Corinthians 5:16 (my translation).
8   Acts 7:60–8:1.
9   Acts 26:10–11; 22:4; 8:3; 9:4; 22:8; cf. Galatians 1:13, 22–23; Philippians 3:6;
    1 Timothy 1:12.

Paul was converted soon after the First Easter

Paul was an early convert to Jesus Christ. He did not, as some infer, become a Christian convert many years after Jesus, but in the period immediately following Jesus. While we cannot date his conversion exactly, it cannot have been much more than a year after the First Easter. Quite possibly it was an even shorter period. How do we know this?

Our calculations are based on two milestones. One is the date of the First Easter at AD 33;[10] the other is Paul's arrival in Corinth in AD 50.[11] Seventeen years separate these two events.

We know quite a lot about Paul in the period between Jesus' Easter in AD 33 and the apostle's coming to Corinth in AD 50. Thirteen to fourteen years after his Damascus Road conversion he attended a missionary meeting in Jerusalem.[12] Between that meeting in Jerusalem and his coming to Corinth a period of about three years must be allowed. If we add to the thirteen to fourteen years between the Damascus Road and the Jerusalem conference the three between Jerusalem and Corinth we reach a sum of between sixteen and seventeen years. But this is the period between Jesus' Easter and Paul's arrival in Corinth. We conclude, therefore, that Paul's Damascus Road conversion occurred in the order of one year, more or less, after Jesus' death and resurrection 3–5 April AD 33. Clearly Paul was a very early convert to Jesus Christ.

---

10 See C.J. Humphreys and W.G. Waddington *Nature* 306 (1983) 743–746; *Nature* 348 (1990) 684.

11 Three factors give us confidence in dating Paul's arrival in Corinth in AD 50: (1) His involvement with Priscilla and Aquila who had been among the Jews expelled from Italy under Claudius (Acts 18:2), which we know from other sources (Suetonius, *Claudius* xxv.4; Orosius, *History* 7.6.15–16) occurred in AD 49, (2) an inscription at Delphi which establishes Gallio's incumbency as Proconsul of Achaia to 1 July AD 51 – 30 June AD 52 (C.K Barrett, *The New Testament Background*, 50; cf. Acts 18:12–17) and (3) the period of his sojourn in Corinth was a year and a half (Acts 18:10).

12 See Galatians 2:1, 7–9. Paul counts first three, then fourteen years from his conversion; everything is calculated from that great turning point. But fourteen years then meant up to fourteen; part-years were counted as full years.

Paul's Letters contain oral history

Modern historians are very interested in oral history. Through the development of audio- and video-taping technology the living voice of people who were present at great events can be heard. Many will have heard the voice of the radio announcer who described the Hindenberg disaster. Who can forget the words that reverberated around the world's airwaves reporting that President Kennedy had been assassinated?

We do not have the technology to recreate the voices of centuries ago, but as it happens, there is embedded within Paul's Letters a number of quotations of those who were believers before Paul, including those who had been disciples of the historical Jesus. Paul's quoted 'traditions' approximate to modern audio-taped extracts and are of enormous historical value as the living voice of the past. Through these we hear, as it were, the oral testimony of those who spoke to Paul about Jesus and, indeed, the words of Jesus himself.

Paul usually introduces these quotations by 'I received...'[13] From whom did Paul 'receive' these 'traditions'? Paul tells us that within three years of the Damascus Road conversion he returned to Jerusalem 'to inquire *(historēsai)* of Cephas (Peter)'. Paul stayed with Peter for fifteen days. This means that Paul was making his own *historical inquiry*[14] about Jesus from one who was in an unparalleled position to supply information about all that Jesus did and taught, as well as what happened to him on Easter Day. It is highly probable that Peter showed Paul the tomb in which Jesus was buried, but which was then empty.

The Apostle goes on to say that he also saw James, the brother of Jesus. In addition to having access to all that Jesus

---

13   1 Corinthians 11:23; 15:1.
14   Galatians 1:18 (my translation). The word 'inquire' translates the Greek *historēsai*, from which the English word 'history' is derived.

did and said during his ministry, Paul also had access to Jesus' home life in Nazareth from the lips of his younger brother, James.

Paul was an early convert to Jesus. Even before his conversion he knew about Jesus, though he took strongest exception to all that he knew about him. Within three years of that conversion he was able to meet Peter, the leading disciple of Jesus, and also James, the Lord's brother. It is clear that Paul had access to extensive and significant information about Jesus.

Paul's Letters are historically close to Jesus

The thirteen Letters of the apostle Paul were written within a known time frame, c. AD 50–65. We can pinpoint Paul's arrival in Corinth to AD 50 when he wrote 1 Thessalonians, in all probability his first letter, though some believe Galatians was written one or two years earlier.[15] At the further extremity, the assault of the Emperor Nero on the Christians of Rome ended the life of the apostle in the mid-sixties.[16]

Since the First Easter is to be dated AD 33, a mere seventeen years – a very short time span – separates the historical Jesus from Paul's arrival in Corinth and the writing of 1 Thessalonians. In comparison, about fifty years elapsed between the death of the Emperor Nero and the writing of our major source of information about him, Tacitus' *Annals of Imperial Rome*.[17] It is difficult to think of a major figure of that period whose primary interpreter is closer to that figure than Paul is to Jesus.

The situation, then, is that Paul's Letters are historically close to Jesus, the nearest being seventeen and the furthest

---

15 That is, in c. AD 48.
16 So the early Christian writers Clement of Rome (*1 Clement* v.vii) and Eusebius (*History of the Church* ii.25.5–8).
17 Nero died AD 68; Tacitus wrote the *Annals of Imperial Rome* c. AD 116.

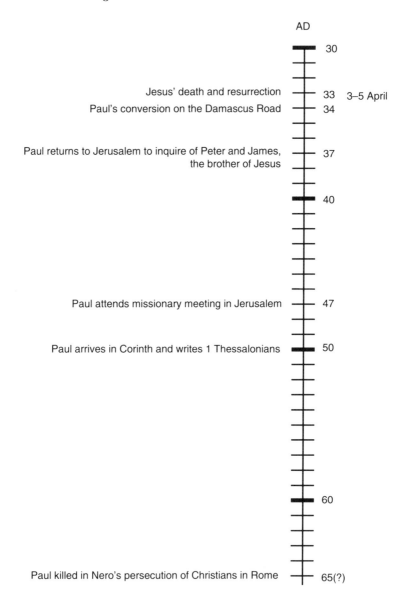

AD

Jesus' death and resurrection — 33   3–5 April
Paul's conversion on the Damascus Road — 34

Paul returns to Jerusalem to inquire of Peter and James,
the brother of Jesus — 37

— 40

Paul attends missionary meeting in Jerusalem — 47

Paul arrives in Corinth and writes 1 Thessalonians — 50

— 60

Paul killed in Nero's persecution of Christians in Rome — 65(?)

Paul's ministry

thirty-two years removed from him. Within those Letters are to be found a number of passages of oral quotations probably derived from Peter and James within three years of Paul's conversion. Even earlier, Paul knew about Jesus from those he persecuted within the first year of the life of the primitive church. It is quite possible that Paul had heard Jesus directly.

Paul's closeness to Jesus is significant, for two reasons: (1) as noted above, Paul had ready access to orally formulated information about Jesus; (2) within so short a period as the three years between the First Easter and Paul's reception of the traditions about Jesus it is unlikely that mythological accretions would have occurred.

WHAT DID PAUL KNOW ABOUT JESUS?

Paul writes his Letters to the churches to deal with problems which were painfully current. He relates those problems to the Jesus contemporary with those situations, that is to Jesus the exalted Lord rather than the historical Jesus. The Gospels direct the reader back to Jesus of Nazareth, Paul directs his readers up to the risen Lord.

Nonetheless, Paul does refer many times to the pre-Easter Jesus. Such references are usually made in passing, on the assumption that the readers know such things, with no need for elaboration.

Concerning Jesus' life

According to Paul:

1   Jesus was a descendant of Abraham the Patriarch of the Jews.[18]

---

18   Galatians 3:16.

2   A direct descendant of King David, Jesus was the Christ, the Messiah of Israel.[19]

3   Jesus 'born of a *woman*' suggests that Paul knows of and confirms the virginal conception of Jesus. Paul's words are in agreement with Matthew's: 'Mary, *of whom* Jesus was born, who is called Christ'. Jesus was born of the woman, Mary, not of her husband Joseph.[20]

4   Jesus was born in poverty.[21]

5   Jesus was 'born under' and lived under Jewish Law.[22]

6   Jesus had a brother named James and other brothers, unnamed.[23]

7   His lifestyle was one of humility and meekness, agreeing with his words recorded in the Gospel, 'I am gentle and lowly in heart'.[24]

8   He washed the feet of his disciples.[25]

9   He instituted a memorial meal on the night when he was betrayed.[26]

10 He was cruelly treated at that time.[27]

11 He gave testimony before Pontius Pilate.[28]

12 He was killed by the Jews of Judaea.[29]

13 He was buried.[30]

14 He was raised on the third day and was seen alive on a number of occasions by many hundreds of witnesses, most of whom are still alive, and therefore able to confirm this.[31]

---

19 Romans 1:3; 1 Corinthians 15:3.
20 Galatians 4:5. According to Matthew 1:16, Joseph is not the father of Jesus, but the husband of Mary, 'of whom Jesus was born'. cf. 1:18; Luke 1:34; 3:23.
21 2 Corinthians 8:9.
22 Galatians 4:5.
23 Galatians 1:19; 1 Corinthians 9:5.
24 2 Corinthians 10:1; Matthew 11:29.
25 1 Timothy 5:10.
26 1 Corinthians 11:23–25.
27 Romans 15:3.
28 1 Timothy 6:13.
29 1 Thessalonians 2:14–15.
30 1 Corinthians 15:4.
31 1 Corinthians 15:4–8.

Concerning Jesus' teaching

Paul's references to Jesus' teachings fall into two main classes: direct quotations of Jesus' words, and more allusive references which are identified as coming from Jesus by statements in the Gospels. These classes of use by Paul of Jesus' words amount to a very considerable knowledge of the Master's teaching. One scholar has estimated that Paul uses or alludes to Jesus' teaching more than one thousand times in the course of his thirteen Letters.[32]

Examples of Paul's quotation of Jesus' teaching include:

1   The permanence of marriage among Jesus' covenant people.[33]
2   Ministers of the Gospel are to be financially supported.[34]
3   Members of the new covenant people are to remember Jesus' death in the meal of bread and wine.[35]
4   That, at the return of the Lord, the catching up of those who are still alive will not precede the resurrection of deceased believers.[36]

Not only do we find direct quotation by Paul of Jesus' words, but among the ethical teachings of the apostle are precepts which appear in the Gospels, although they were probably not yet in their final written form. Paul probably had access to Jesus' teachings either through oral tradition or, more probably, through early written collections of Jesus' teachings and sayings. The following are a few examples of words of Paul which derive from Jesus:

1   Forgive, do not avenge, those who persecute you or perpetrate other evil towards you.[37]

---

32   See in W.D. Davies, *Paul and Rabbinic Judaism* (London, SPCK, 1963), 136–143.
33   1 Corinthians 7:10–11; cf. Mark 10:1–12.
34   1 Corinthians 9:14; cf. Luke 10:7; Matthew 10:10–12.
35   1 Corinthians 11:23–25; cf. Mark 14:22–25.
36   1 Thessalonians 4:16; cf. Matthew 24:31.
37   Romans 12:14–21; cf. Matthew 5:44.

2 Pay tax and render honour to civil authorities.[38]
3 Love one another.[39]
4 Why do you judge your brother?[40]
5 There is nothing unclean of itself.[41]
6 Be at peace among yourselves.[42]
7 Continue in prayer and watchfulness.[43]

The list could be extended. But enough has been cited to demonstrate Paul's extensive knowledge of the teachings of Jesus.

One striking characteristic of Paul's citations is their discontinuity with his attitudes as a former Pharisee and zealous persecutor. The forgiveness and the love of Jesus towards the man who is now a believer have had a revolutionary impact on his own sense of values and morality. The radical ethical change reflected in these exhortations is itself evidence of his own conversion to the one 'who loved [him] and gave himself for [him]'.[44]

THE VALUE OF PAUL'S EVIDENCE FOR JESUS

The evidence from Paul about Jesus is, by any criteria, excellent:

1 It is written close in time to Jesus, closer, perhaps than the interpretation for any significant person of the period.
2 It includes oral information going back to Jesus and from the period immediately after Jesus. It resembles oral history which is now seen as especially valuable.

---

38 Romans 13:1–7; Mark 12:13–17.
39 Romans 13:8; cf. Mark 12:28–34.
40 Romans 14:10; cf. Matthew 7:1.
41 Romans 14:14; cf. Mark 7:15.
42 1 Thessalonians 5:13; cf. Mark 9:50.
43 Colossians 4:2; Mark 14:38.
44 Galatians 2:20.

3   It is often information given by way of reminder, only incidentally introduced, to reinforce or to change current attitudes or actions within the churches. It is not evidence given in order to prove the truth claims about Jesus. (Much of the information in the New Testament about such critical elements as the deity of Jesus or his resurrection is introduced gratuitously. These things are not part of the presentation of the moment, but are well established truths that do not have to be argued for, which are only introduced because they are so well known, in order to underpin some current matter. I use the word 'gratuitous' as it is sometimes used with regard to violence in movies or books. The violence is not central to the story line. The story would not be affected if it were omitted.)

4   It is evidence from one who had been a deadly opponent of Jesus and his followers. Thus it fills out and strengthens evidence of those who had, from the beginning, been the followers of Jesus, as set out in the Gospels.

The evidence provided by Paul makes nonsense of those who wish to dismiss the life, teaching, death and resurrection of Jesus as portrayed in the Gospels. Paul's evidence is extensive, early and gratuitous. Significantly, Paul's Letters are, as a corpus, precisely datable to the decade and a half beginning c. AD 50. Moreover, much of it is not unique to him. At many points he is quoting the views of others before him, going back to Jesus. Paul is a major guardian of the historical integrity of Jesus himself.

QUESTIONS FOR REFLECTION AND DISCUSSION:

1. What opportunities would there have been for Paul to have known about Jesus at the time of Jesus' ministry?

2. What is the significance of the brief time-frame between Jesus and Paul's first visit to Jerusalem to inquire of Peter and to see James?

3. What do you say about the claim that Paul perverted the teachings of Jesus?

4. How is Paul significant for our view of the historical Jesus?

FURTHER READING:

P.W. Barnett, *The Two Faces of Jesus* (Sydney, Hodder & Stoughton, 1990).

M. Hengel, *Between Jesus and Paul* (London, SCM, 1981).

Chapter Four

Truth from the Gospels

The Gospels are our major source of information about Jesus. But how reliable are they?

Those who are sceptical about the truth claims about Jesus argue that the Gospels are remote in time from Jesus, that they are written by people who did not know him and that, therefore, the documents are untrustworthy sources of evidence about him. For this reason it will be important to establish when the Gospels were written, by whom, and for what purpose so that we can evaluate the evidence they provide for Jesus.

As with the Letters of Paul, in this inquiry we will treat the Gospels as if they are ordinary documents of history and not as the inspired Word of God. Certainly, if one comes to accept the truth claims about Jesus and accepts the personal authority of Jesus in one's life then a respectful attitude to the scriptures will follow, because that is Jesus' own attitude. But for the time being we will regard the Gospels as generally on a par with, for example, Josephus the Jewish historian who wrote at about the same time as Matthew, Mark, Luke and John and in the same language, Greek.

WHEN WERE THE GOSPELS WRITTEN?

We are able to set early and late limits, AD 33 and AD 100. Since the Gospels look back to Jesus they must have been written after AD 33, the date of the First Easter. On the other hand they must have been in circulation well before AD 100 because they begin to be quoted in books like the Revelation, the First Letter of Clement and the Letters of Ignatius which are known to have been written before, or soon after, the end of the first century. We can be confident that the Gospels were written – to state the matter conservatively – within the six decades following Jesus.

Is it possible to be more precise? The answer is that we cannot be sure exactly when the Gospels were written, apart from the AD 33–100 time frame. The Gospels do not say when they were written and there is no unambiguous external evidence.

Although it is admittedly conjectural, this writer believes the Gospels were written between c. AD 60 to c. AD 70. The Gospels reveal mature reflection about Jesus, the kind of reflection which assumes the perspectives that only distance can give, hence the arbitrary choice of AD 60. Could any one write about Jesus with the appreciation of the Gospel writers closer to him than thirty years? Moreover, had the Gospels been written earlier we would have expected Paul to have quoted more directly from them.

The nomination of AD 70 as an outer limit is more objective. In that year the most horrific event of the century, and of the entire sweep of Jewish history to that point occurred: the final Roman assault on Jerusalem and the destruction of their massive sacred shrine, the Temple built by Herod. Since three of the four Gospels were written by Jews – only Luke was a Gentile – it would be hard to believe that so monumental a tragedy would not have left its imprint within the Gospels, had they been written after AD 70.

Jesus did, indeed, prophesy the Temple's desecration by the 'desolating sacrilege' followed by its destruction.[1] Had the Gospels been written after AD 70, it is likely that the evangelists would have made more of Jesus' prophecy and

1   Mark 13:14–23.

54

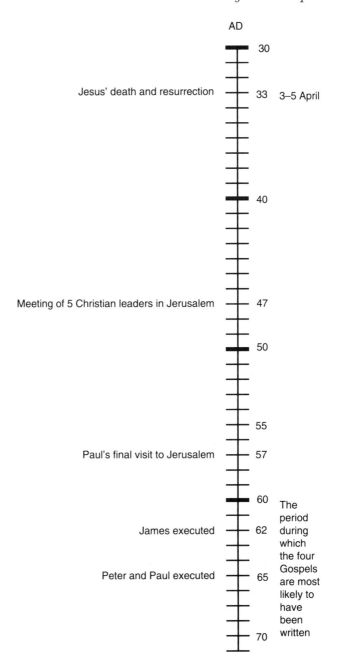

AD

30

Jesus' death and resurrection — 33   3–5 April

40

Meeting of 5 Christian leaders in Jerusalem — 47

50

55

Paul's final visit to Jerusalem — 57

60   The period during which the four Gospels are most likely to have been written

James executed — 62

Peter and Paul executed — 65

70

they would have tidied up the details of the sequence. The minor imprecision in Jesus' prophecy is an evidence of its historical veracity. Significantly, the historian Josephus, who was present with the Roman commander Titus as an eyewitness, describes the events in reverse order. The Romans desecrated the sacred precinct after it had been substantially destroyed.[2]

It is reasonable to suggest, therefore, that the four Gospels were *completed* between c. AD 60 and c. AD 70, that is, between thirty and forty years after Jesus.

WHY WERE THE GOSPELS WRITTEN?

It would be more accurate to ask, 'Why were the Gospels *completed*?'

Luke tells us that initially the original eyewitnesses of Jesus wrote about particular phases of Jesus' ministry, which they 'delivered' to him and which he then consolidated into the one complete, continuous narrative.[3] The careful comparison of the sayings of Jesus recorded in Matthew and Luke suggests that both those writers had access to independent earlier written collections of Jesus' teachings which they incorporated within their Gospels.

We can readily understand how this compilation would come about:

At first, travelling apostles and evangelists would come to a town and tell people the message about Jesus. Churches were established based on a *spoken* ministry. These preachers moved on for ministry elsewhere, but the churches they established needed to have permanent information about Jesus. Thus from quite early within the history of the primitive churches brief *written* resources telling of Jesus'

---

2   *Jewish War* vi.316.
3   Luke 1:1–4.

words and deeds were compiled, copied and made available for local use.

But the churches were surrounded by unhelpful cultural pressure, whether Jewish or Gentile. Wrong attitudes to Jesus and to fellow members would begin to develop within the churches. When these came to the attention of Christian leaders various measures would be adopted. Perhaps a leader would make a follow up visit to set the wrongs right. Also, the leaders of early Christianity made much use of the Epistle, the formal letter, which would be sent either to an individual church or as a circular to a cluster of churches within an apostle's sphere of missionary activity.

A final development then occurred. Various versions of brief pre-formed data about Jesus – oral as well as written – were incorporated within *completed* documents, which we know as the Gospels of Matthew, Mark, Luke and John. (As stated above, these Gospels appear to have reached their final form in the period between AD 60 and AD 70.)

What circumstances arose during this period of time which led to the creation of four completed, written Gospels? It was within this span that the majority of the leaders of the various mission groups were killed. James, leader of a mission to Jews, was executed in AD 62;[4] Peter, leader of a mission to Jews and Gentiles, was executed in c. AD 65; and Paul, Apostle to the Gentiles, was executed in c. AD 65.[5] The removal of these great mission leaders James, Peter and Paul hastened the gathering and ordering of Gospels from more fragmentary materials used by or known to these missions. The deaths of the mission leaders, more than any other factor, prompted the completion of the Gospels.

Thus there are two kinds of literature in the New Testament. One is the Gospel, the Jesus biography. There

---

4   Josephus, *Antiquities of the Jews*, xx.200.
5   Eusebius, *Historia Ecclesia* II.25.5-8; cf. 1 Clement v.vi.

are four of these Gospels – According to Matthew, According to Mark, According to Luke (written in two parts, one about Jesus pre-Easter, the other – the Book of Acts – about Jesus post-Easter) and According to John.

The other kind is the Epistle or Letter of which there are twenty-two: one by James, two by Peter, thirteen by Paul, four by John (including his extended Letter – the Book of Revelation) and one each by the anonymous writer of Hebrews and Jude.

The Letters were written before the Gospels were completed, though it is likely that preliminary portions of the Gospels were circulated separately before the Letters were written.

FOUR MISSION LEADERS; FOUR GOSPELS

In c. AD 47, five Christian leaders met privately in Jerusalem.[6] Three – James, Cephas (Peter) and John – were the 'pillars' of the Church of Jerusalem and two – Barnabas and Paul – were leaders from the Church of Antioch, in northern Syria. The Church of Jerusalem, holding primacy of honour, agreed that the delegates from Antioch should *go* to the Gentiles, while the Jerusalem 'pillars' should *go* to the Jews.[7] There would thus be two missions (literally 'apostolates', or '*sent*-missions'), which were not defined by geography but by ethnicity.

Paul's apostolate to the Gentiles is well-known to us through his own Letters and the space devoted to his ministry in the Acts of the Apostles, where he is the chief character. The other mission, focused on Jews, is chiefly known from Paul's final visit to Jerusalem in c. AD 57 when the Elders and *James* pointed to 'many thousands' of believers among the Jews.[8]

---

6   Galatians 2:7–9.
7   Galatians 2:1–2, 6–9.
8   Acts 21:20.

In the years after the Jerusalem meeting, two other ministries evolved, one associated with *Peter,* the other associated with *John.* Direct evidence for these ministries, however, is fragmentary. We know of Peter's ministry from (1) scattered references to him in the Acts, which, however, terminate c. AD 49,[9] (2) information gleaned from the two Letters bearing his name and (3) from the post-apostolic writers. Even less is known of John. The Acts makes no reference to John later than the mid-thirties. Apart from the mention of his name in Galatians 2, nothing direct is known of John until the post-apostolic period.

That Peter and John engaged in ministries independent of James, however, is to be be inferred from the literature associated with them. The literature was produced for the churches associated with the ministries of Peter and John. Whereas Paul's mission was chiefly to Gentiles and James' exclusively to Jews, Peter's and John's ministries appear to have encompassed both Jews and Gentiles, with increasing emphasis upon Gentiles. The two Letters of Peter and the Gospel of Mark supply the evidence of Peter's ministry and the three Letters of John, the Gospel bearing his name and the Revelation suggest that there was a ministry to churches led by John Zebedee, the 'beloved disciple'.

It is important to recognise that these four leaders did not work in isolation, but with support teams. All the evidence points to groups of fellow-workers who actively shared in ministry activity associated with the leader. Indeed, some of the associates were significant leaders in their own right; Luke and Mark, for example, were responsible for the writing of a Gospel for the mission churches of their leader:

- Luke, Paul's esteemed colleague, wrote the Gospel of Luke and the Acts of the Apostles out of and to extend the great mission work of Paul, Apostle to the Gentiles.

---

9 Acts 15:7–11.

- Mark, who had acted as interpreter to Greek-speaking audiences for Peter's Aramaic preaching, wrote his Gospel on the basis of his own recollections of Peter's words.
- Matthew's Gospel, which appears to arise out of James' mission work to Palestinian Jews, is written by one who had been a Galilean disciple of Jesus.
- The Gospel and the Letters of John, along with the Revelation, are the work of the 'beloved disciple' himself.

If the four Gospels arise out of the ministries of four Christian leaders, where were they written?

- Matthew, drawing on material appropriate to Palestinian Jewish churches, may have written his Gospel in Galilee.
- Mark appears to have written his Gospel in Rome, for Gentile subjects of the Roman Emperor, to commend God's true King, the crucified Son of God.
- It is believed that Luke wrote his two-volumed work in Caesarea for 'Godfearer' (Gentile members of Jewish synagogues) and Gentile readers.
- John, whose Revelation is directed to the churches of Asia, probably wrote his Gospel from Ephesus, the major city of the Roman province of Asia.

The Gospels were not confined to readers in these particular centres of Christianity, but were circulated among the churches associated with the missions and ministries of the great leaders, wherever those churches may have been. The Gospels were the last testimony of the great mission leaders – Peter, John, James and Paul – to the churches of their missions.

THE AUTHENTICITY OF GOSPEL EVIDENCE

What, then, do we say to the claim that the Gospels are

remote in time, cut off from Jesus and therefore essentially unreliable?

Our response is that, on the contrary, the Gospel evidence is, historically speaking, very impressive: (1) The Gospels were written within living memory of Jesus. (2) Two of the Gospels (Matthew and John) were written by disciples and eyewitnesses of Jesus. The other two (Mark and Luke) were written by those who were dependent on and in touch with eyewitnesses. (3) There are no less than four Gospels, giving a breadth of independent testimony to Jesus.

The completed documents – Matthew, Mark, Luke and John – were written by those who were directly, or, at most at one remove, connected to Jesus. The authors, whose integrity is authenticated by this historical connection with Jesus, used living mission material.

The Jewish ethos: the Gospels are in living contact with Jesus

It must be remembered that the four mission leaders who met in Jerusalem c. AD 47 – James, Peter, John and Paul – were Jews.

Jewish culture was at that time profoundly rabbi-centred. The rabbi would carefully instruct the pupil-rabbi, who would then, as a rabbi, teach his pupils. Much of this instruction was by rote learning. The rabbi would 'hand over' and the pupil would 'receive' his teachings which were known as 'traditions',[10] which would, in turn be handed over to a pupil. And so on. These teachers formed a chain of living links; they were not cut off from each other.

This is precisely the culture whose practice and vocabulary were reproduced in the early decades of Christianity. The Father 'handed over' his teaching to Jesus who, in turn, told his 'disciples' (pupils): 'Take my yoke on

---

10 For evidence of 'traditions' which were 'handed on' and 'received' among the Jews see Mark 7:1–9 and Galatians 1:14.

you, learn from me.'[11] The disciples call him 'Rabbi' and they 'follow' him.

In the immediate post-Easter period, Jesus' Galilean followers chose from among their number a twelfth apostle (to replace Judas who had committed suicide);[12] the essential qualification was that he had accompanied Jesus from the time of John's baptism of him until his ascension.[13] The first converts of post-Easter Christianity devoted themselves to the 'apostles' teaching',[14] doctrines which they had received from their Teacher in the pre-Easter period.

Likewise, the apostle Paul, upon establishing the churches through his preaching, 'hands over' to them oral 'traditions' which they 'receive', and which he himself had 'received' earlier from apostles like Peter and James, the brother of the Lord.[15]

The vocabulary of the rabbinic teacher and the transmission of his teaching is very common in the New Testament. Repeatedly, congregations are encouraged to 'hold', 'keep', 'walk according to' or 'guard' the 'tradition' or 'the pattern of teaching' or 'the faith' which had been 'delivered to' them and which they have 'received'.[16]

Thus the Gospels arose in a rabbinic milieu of 'passed-on' traditions. They were completed by those who were joined by a living link with Jesus whether directly and primarily, in the case of Matthew and John, or indirectly and secondarily, in the case of Mark and Luke. The Gospels are not dry and lifeless documents cut off from Jesus; they are part of his living flesh and blood.

This Jewish ethos of living links in a chain may still be detected a century later than Jesus. In the first quarter of the

---

11 Matthew 11:29.
12 Matthew 27:3–10.
13 Acts 1:21–26.
14 Acts 2:42; 6:4.
15 1 Thessalonians 2:13; 4:1; 2 Thessalonians 2:15; 1 Corinthians 11:2, 23; 15:1–5; Galatians 1:18–19.
16 See e.g. Romans 6:17; Jude 3.

next century, Papias, Bishop of Hierapolis in Asia Minor, was in contact with those he calls 'followers', that is, followers of those who learned from the 'elders', the original disciples of the Lord. Papias would go to these 'followers' to find out what the 'elders' had taught. Papias regarded this 'living and abiding voice' as 'the guarantee of truth'.

Papias is in contact with the 'elders' (Jesus' disciples) through contact with their followers. With the passage of time, the living contact with the fountainhead is diminished. But the Gospels, which are removed from him by forty years or less, are in living contact with Jesus, through his disciples and their mission associates.

The Four Gospels

The second century was a time of theological confusion. The rise of Gnosticism with its publication of spurious Gospels made it necessary for orthodox Christians to declare that there were only four authentic Gospels. Early manuscripts of the Gospels are headed 'According to Matthew', 'According to Mark', 'According to Luke' and 'According to John'. The Christians of the second century were adamant: there were *four* Gospels and these were their authors.[17]

But did these men – Matthew, Mark, Luke and John – actually write the Gospels? Apart from the fourth Gospel, which declares itself to be written by the 'beloved disciple',[18] these books do not identify their authors. Nonetheless, the case for genuineness of authorship is strong.

Early and independent evidence from all quarters points to four Gospels 'according to' these four men. The names of

---

17 *Four* Gospels are specified by (1) The Muratorian Canon, a list of books of the New Testament which was accepted in the church in Rome in the second century, (2) the Anti-Marcionite prologue to the Gospel of Luke, believed to have originated in the second century and (3) the second century writer Irenaeus, *Against Heresies* III.11.11, III.11.8.

18 John 21:20, 24; cf. 19:35.

these four is a further factor. Had the Gospels borne the names of well-known figures like Peter, James and Paul we may, perhaps, have been suspicious, as indeed we are of later Gnostic works supposedly written by Peter and others who are so prominent in the New Testament. But, apart from John, the writers Matthew, Mark and Luke are relatively minor figures in the New Testament. Their relative inferiority strengthens the case for their authenticity.

These four Gospels bear a close association with the four missions which evolved from the meeting in Jerusalem c. AD 47. The Gospel 'according to Matthew' appears to be connected with James, that 'according to Mark' with Peter, that 'according to Luke' with Paul and that 'according to John' with John Zebedee, the 'beloved disciple'. These Gospels represent, in finished form, mission literature about Jesus associated with the apostolates of these great leaders.

Matthew

Second-century writers unanimously refer to the first of the four Gospels as 'according to Matthew'. This 'Matthew' must be the apostle of that name, who appears in the list of the twelve apostles in the Gospel of Matthew.[19] Based on references in the Gospel of Mark, this 'Matthew' is to be identified as Levi, a wealthy tax collector from Capernaum whom Jesus called to follow him.[20] Possibly his full name was Matthew the Levite, son of Alphaeus.

Matthew's own role in the writing of the Gospel bearing his name is uncertain. Various underlying sources have been identified, including the Gospel of Mark, which supplies the basic narrative of events. Inserted into this framework are teachings of Jesus derived from collections known as 'Q' and

---

19 Matthew 10:3.
20 Matthew 9:9; cf. Mark 2:14–17. Tax collecting was lucrative. Levi must have been a man of means to provide hospitality in his house to 'many tax collectors' as well as Jesus and his disciples.

'M'.[21] It is possible that Matthew had also been responsible for compiling one or other of these earlier collections of sayings. Papias states that Matthew 'compiled the oracles [of the Lord] in the Hebrew language'.[22] The universal tradition of the second century attributing the first Gospel to Matthew suggests that Matthew wrote the finished work 'According to Matthew'.

But would Matthew, who had been a disciple, have used the narrative of another, that is, of the Gospel of Mark? Writing was a laborious and very expensive process at that time. If someone else had created an acceptable account, there was no practical or moral reason not to adapt it and add to it. It must not be forgotten that Mark's narrative arises from Peter's preaching about the ministry of Jesus. Matthew has taken Mark's splendid Gospel, shortened it at many points and, by adding other source material to it, has created his own remarkable Gospel. Many composers, Brahms and Liszt, for example, have used music written by others as a basis for a new masterpiece.[23]

Judaea and Galilee, the world of Matthew's Gospel where Jesus comes before us, is an exclusively Jewish world. Gentiles surround it and, on occasion, like the Magi, enter it. Gentiles will, in the Last Day, stream into Israel from 'east and west'.[24] In this Gospel, practices unique to Jews are referred to, but never explained. For the duration of his ministry Jesus and his disciples were to 'go nowhere among the Gentiles' but to confine themselves to the 'lost sheep of the house of Israel'. Only after the resurrection are the apostles to 'go' outside Israel to the Gentiles to make

---

21 'Q', from the German *Quelle* ('source') is a collection apparently used by both Matthew and Luke; 'M' and 'L' are collections of Jesus' teachings found only in Matthew and Luke respectively.
22 Eusebius, *Historia Ecclesia* III.39.16.
23 Peter, in his Second Letter, appears to have incorporated the Letter of Jude. Today an author would acknowledge his dependence on the works of others. But this is a modern development.
24 Matthew 8:11–12.

disciples of Jesus the Messiah.[25] Culturally speaking, Matthew's is the most Jewish of the four Gospels, written – so it appears – for Jewish Christian readers.

It seems likely, therefore, that Matthew was closely connected with James, the Jerusalem-based leader of the mission to the Jews c. AD 41–62. Many of the teachings of the Letter of James – for example, about God as a generous father, the need not merely to hear but to do the word, the plight of the hungry, the effects of wrong speech, the evils of judging others, the ban on oaths – echo the teachings of Jesus as recorded in the Gospel of Matthew.[26]

On the other hand, Matthew appears to place great emphasis on Galilee, which is understandable since Matthew began to follow Jesus in Capernaum in Galilee. According to Matthew, it was when Jesus began his ministry in Capernaum – in 'Galilee of the Gentiles' – that God shone his great light for the sake of those who sat in darkness and the shadow of death.[27] It was from Galilee that the apostles were to take the Gospel of the risen Messiah to the nations of the world, the Gentiles.[28] From Matthew's perspective, Galilee is the centre for the world mission to the nations.[29]

As the following schema indicates, the Gospel of Matthew flowed from a living contact with Jesus:

Jesus----Levi/Matthew----------Matthew: The Gospel----------------------------James
According to Matthew

Mark

The second Gospel mentioned in the second century, 'According to Mark', also has a living connection with Jesus, though a secondary and indirect one.

---

25 Matthew 10:5–6; 28:19.
26 See P.W. Barnett, *Bethlehem to Patmos* (Sydney, Hodder & Stoughton, 1989), 201.
27 Matthew 4:15–17.
28 Matthew 28:16–20.
29 Matthew 4:24–25.

This 'Mark' is the John Mark whom we encounter in the New Testament. The Gospel 'according to Mark', like the other three, arose out of one of the four missions, that associated with Peter. Thus like the other three Gospels, the second Gospel flows from living contact with Jesus.

Mark's relationship with Peter spans at least thirty years. It first comes into view in Jerusalem in c. AD 41 where Peter's ministry is associated with the home of Mark's mother. It is last seen in 'Babylon', a coded reference to Rome, where Peter sends greetings to the churches of Asia Minor on behalf of 'my son, Mark'.[30] In the period between those extremities we catch glimpses of Mark in mission work in Cyprus and southern Asia Minor, first with his cousin Barnabas, and Paul, and then with Barnabas alone in Cyprus.[31]

Papias, the Bishop of Hierapolis in Asia Minor, was taught by John the Elder, who in turn had been instructed by the apostles of the Lord. Papias relates the words of this John about the Gospel of Mark:

> Mark...having been the interpreter of Peter, wrote accurately...all that he recalled of what was either said or done by the Lord...[Mark] was...a follower...of Peter.[32]

Following the rabbinical ethos, Mark was a disciple of Peter who was a disciple of the Lord. Peter, the mission leader, has Mark as his interpreter of his teaching about Jesus.

Consistent with its association with Peter the eyewitness, the Gospel of Mark proves to be extraordinarily vivid and colourful, especially in its record of human and emotional detail. Through Mark's written words we hear, at first hand,

---

30 Acts 12:12; 1 Peter 5:13.
31 Acts 12:25; 13:5, 13; 15:39–40.
32 Eusebius, *Historia Ecclesiastica* III.39.15.

Peter's stories of Jesus' lively encounters with the procession of characters who come to him.[33]

The connection between Mark and the First Letter of Peter may be noted by the occurrence of vocabulary and ideas common to both. For example, Jesus' teaching about himself as a *ransom* recorded in Mark is echoed in 1 Peter.[34] Likewise Jesus' quotation of Psalm 118 regarding the stone that was to be *rejected,* but which was to be the cornerstone of the new temple, is found in Mark and is also echoed in 1 Peter.[35] Jesus' observations about *domineering* Gentile rulers recorded in Mark are applied in 1 Peter as a warning to church elders.[36] A particular nexus exists between 1 Peter and Mark which is consistent with a mission associate (Mark) reflecting the same ideas as the mission leader (Peter), which in turn derive from the Master.

As the following schema shows, the Gospel according to Mark is written in living contact with Jesus, through Mark's discipleship of Peter, the disciple of the Lord:

Jesus-----------Peter-------------------------------- Mark: The Gospel According to Mark

Luke

Independently of each other, the orthodox writers of the second century identify the author of the third Gospel as Luke the physician, the companion of Paul. Once again, a Gospel is closely associated with a mission leader, in this case Paul, apostle to the Gentiles.

In the opening words of his Gospel, Luke makes clear that his own relationship with Jesus is not that of an eyewitness: '...many who from the beginning were eyewitnesses and ministers of the word and have compiled

---

33 See P.W. Barnett, *Is the New Testament History?* (Sydney, Hodder & Stoughton, 1986), 81–98.
34 Mark 10:45; 1 Peter 1:18.
35 Mark 12:10–11; 8:31; 1 Peter 2:4.
36 Mark 10:42; 1 Peter 5:3.

narratives about Jesus have delivered them to me.' Luke makes it clear that although he was not an eyewitness, he was in contact with Jesus through those who were, from the beginning, eyewitnesses. These 'eyewitnesses and ministers of the word' – that is, the original disciples – have 'handed over' to Luke various written narratives about Jesus from which he has, in turn, written his 'orderly account'.[37]

Once again the rabbinic vocabulary is used. These eyewitnesses have 'handed over' to Luke written information about Jesus which arose from their direct contact with him, establishing the integrity of Luke's Gospel.

As with the other Gospels, the written Gospel 'according to Luke' has a living contact with Jesus, in this case through those who 'from the beginning were eyewitnesses and ministers of the word' to Luke the author.

Jesus------Eyewitnesses--------------------Luke: The Gospel----------------------------Paul
According to Luke

John

The orthodox writers of the second century identify the Gospel 'according to John' as the work of John Zebedee, the beloved disciple.[38] The Gospel itself declares its authorship. Referring to 'the disciple whom Jesus loved', the final verses of the Fourth Gospel state: 'This is the disciple who testifies to these things and who wrote them down'.[39]

In his First Letter and in his Gospel, this writer claims to have touched, seen and heard Jesus and to have been present when he died on the cross.[40] The Letters and the Gospel of John have much in common – for example, the

---

37 Luke 1:1–3 (my translation).
38 Irenaeus, *Against Heresies* III.1.1. Irenaeus was in contact with Polycarp who was in contact with people from the apostolic age, including John (III.3.4).
39 John 21:20, 24.
40 1 John 1:1–3; John 19:35. It is clear – by a process of elimination – that the beloved disciple must be John Zebedee; see John 21:2; cf. 13:23–24.

parallel contrasts between light and darkness, life and death and allusions to the water and the blood. Clearly, the Letters and Gospel arise from the one source.

Moreover, added to the beloved disciple's own eyewitness claim is the affidavit of the apostolic community: '*We* know that his testimony is true.'[41] Earlier in this Gospel the 'we'/'us' are identified as the disciples who had been present with Jesus and seen his glory.[42] The writer speaks on his own behalf knowing that his fellow-witnesses confirm the truth of what he says.

Like Matthew, but unlike Mark and Luke, John had been in direct and immediate living contact with Jesus. Unlike Matthew, however, who appears to use other sources (as well as his own?) in completing the finished Gospel, John's Gospel appears to use his own material; no non-Johannine sources are evident.

The Gospel 'according to John' is the most fact-specific of the four Gospels. When it comes to precision of references to the passage of time or the names of people and of places and of towns, this Gospel is unparalleled, which is the more remarkable in light of the powerful theological terms in which it is written.[43]

The schema is revealing; no intermediaries separate this author from Jesus:

Jesus-------------John--The Gospel According to John

John makes direct claim to be an eyewitness to Jesus' miracles, his death, the emptiness of the tomb and the fact of the resurrection.[44] At the end of the Gospel there is this postscript: 'We know that his testimony is true.'[45] John's

---

41 John 21:24.
42 John 1:14; 2:11.
43 See P.W. Barnett, *Is the New Testament History?* (Sydney, Hodder & Stoughton, 1986), 59–79.
44 John 1:14; 2:11; 19:35; 20:8; 20:19–23.
45 John 21:24.

witness is authenticated by others ('we') who were the disciples of the Lord.[46]

The assertion that the Gospels are late in time and cut off from Jesus is incorrect. All the evidence points to the Gospels being written in living reach of Jesus by those who were his immediate followers, or by those who were associates of the original disciples.

The references to the transmission of teaching from teacher to pupil along Jewish lines enables us to establish this living relationship with Jesus. In the case of Mark and Luke it was at one remove from Jesus, through those who were the direct companions of the Lord. In the case of Matthew and John the contact was immediate and direct.

The Gospels were written out of and for the mission activities of groups led by James, Peter, Paul and John. But in no case is the written material cut off from a living relationship with Jesus, indirect or direct.

Jesus			
Mission leader	James	Peter	John	Paul
Mission target	Jews	Jews and then Gentiles	Jews and then Gentiles	Gentiles
Gospel author	Matthew	Mark	John	Luke
Where written	Galilee?	Rome?	Ephesus?	Caesarea?

Genuine and reliable evidence for Jesus is found on every page of the Gospels. Such confidence as now expressed is

---

46 John 1:14; 2:11.

not an act of faith in the divine inspiration of the Gospels —
worthy of such faith as they may be — but rather in their
intrinsically historical character.

	Contact with Jesus	Author	Gospel
Jesus	Matthew	Matthew	According to Matthew
	Peter	Mark	According to Mark
	John	John	According to John
	original disciples	Luke	According to Luke

QUESTIONS FOR REFLECTION AND DISCUSSION:

1. What is the Jewish ethos in which the Gospels were
   produced, and why is this important for their
   authenticity?

2. What do you say to those who claim the Gospels are
   remote in time and cut off from Jesus?

3. Discuss the relationship between the various mission
   teams and the Gospels.

FURTHER READING:

C. Blomberg, *The Historical Reliability of the Gospels* (Leicester, IVP, 1987).

B. Gerhardsson, *The Origins of the Gospel Traditions* (London, SCM, 1979).

J.A.T. Robinson, *Redating the New Testament* (London, SCM, 1976).

Chapter Five

Truth about Jesus, God's Special Man

Jesus was crucified in AD 33, leaving behind a hundred or so Galilean followers in Jerusalem. Yet within three decades this movement had become so numerous in Rome, and such a perceived threat, that the Emperor Nero – to deflect suspicion from himself – was able to make scapegoats of the Christians.

By that time congregations devoted to the worship of Jesus had been established in the cities and towns that ringed the shores of the eastern Mediterranean, as well as many inland centres. There are many indications that these congregations, with their beliefs about Jesus, made their presence felt locally. So overt was their commitment to Christ that the people of Antioch called them *Christianoi* 'Christians'.[1]

Paul's impact on the cult of Artemis, the patron deity of the city of Ephesus, was so great that a city-wide demonstration against him was held in the great amphitheatre.[2] In Bithynia, on the southern shores of the Black Sea, the mass conversions of local people effectively closed the local temples and the businesses of those who sold animals for sacrifice.[3]

Such was the phenomenal success of the early missions, led by James, Peter, John and Paul and by others whose names have not survived.

---

1   Acts 11:26.
2   Acts 19:23–27.
3   Pliny, *Epistle* 10.96.

74

This widening and strengthening of Christianity is a secure fact of history.

THE MISSION LETTERS

Contemporary evidence of those missions is afforded by the Letters of James, Peter, John and Paul, as well as by the Letter to the Hebrews and the Letter of Jude, which are part of the New Testament. Letters do, indeed, provide contemporary evidence. By nature, a letter deals with current matters, the things of now.

The Letters from the mission leaders to the churches are 'follow up' Letters, reminding and reinforcing what had already been communicated verbally by the evangelists who established the churches. They rarely introduce doctrines which had not been taught earlier, though they often correct distortions of belief and practice which have arisen in the meantime.

Honest inquirers into the truth claims of Jesus should be very interested in these mission Letters. The information they yield about Jesus was not given to convince the undecided, but to confirm the already decided in the commitment they have made. Such Jesus-data is, therefore, gratuitous and innocently given, and of great interest to both honest inquirers into the claims of Jesus as well as to professional historians of Christian origins.

THE 'MESSAGE' IN THE LETTERS

We discover from the mission Letters that congregations were formed as people heard a verbally given *message* about Jesus. From these Letters we are able to piece together some of the elements fundamental to the beliefs of the early churches. These include:

1   God's long-awaited last day has dawned
2   in the coming, death and resurrection of God's Special Man, Jesus,
3   who will return, bringing history to its appointed end.

The following table of examples illustrates these relationships:

Letters	James	Peter	John	Paul
1. God's long-awaited last day has dawned		1 Peter 1:10–12		Romans 1:2
2. In the sending/ coming of God's Special Man		1 Peter 1:19–20	1 John 1:1–3	Romans 1:3–4
3. Who will return bringing history to an end.	James 5:9, 15	1 Peter 1:13	1 John 3:2	1 Thess. 4:14–15

The Gospel in the Letters

Not only is this Jesus-data innocently and gratuitously given, it is also *independently* given; the Letters of the different mission leaders, James, Peter, John and Paul were not written in collaboration. It must be regarded as a secure fact of history that the beliefs of the mission congregations about Jesus followed these lines.

WHY WERE THE GOSPELS NEEDED?

If the mission Letters were written to reinforce and remind

the churches about the faith, why were Gospels also needed?

In the previous chapter, one reason given for the writing of the Gospels was the passing of the great mission leaders James, Peter and Paul in the sixties. The living contact was being lost. Permanent and authentic narratives about Jesus were needed.

There is a further, closely connected, reason. Churches and Christians needed to know more about the Man in whom they had believed. They needed expanded, 'fleshed out' narrative about him. The oral tradition and the short collections of Jesus' sayings and teachings needed to be ordered and consolidated.

It is probable, too, that the rise during the fifties and sixties of Gnosticism – the mythical and mystical outlook which was opposed to this world and therefore to the notion of time and space – may have created an an anti-historical 'climate'. It was important for the apostles to establish that Jesus was indeed a real person of history, a man of flesh and blood, and not merely a time-less and space-less 'idea', who had redemptive power.

THE 'MESSAGE' IN THE GOSPELS

When we turn to the Gospels of the four missions we find a similar threefold pattern of teaching about Jesus, as in the Letters. The Gospels, however, do not merely re-state these doctrines, but give fleshed out narratives about Jesus.

1   God's long-awaited day has dawned

The beginning of each Gospel establishes that God is now fulfilling all the expectations raised by the prophets in the Old Testament. This is now the beginning of God's final chapter. God's great light has shone on the peoples of the world as they sit in darkness and the shadow of death. This day has now dawned.

Prominent at the beginning of each Gospel is John the Baptist, the long-awaited forerunner prophesied in the Old Testament, who points to Jesus as the Greater One who is to come, who will baptise with the Holy Spirit.

Following immediately after John the Baptist, Jesus declares that the time is now fulfilled, that God is about to break into history and establish his Kingdom. Let Israel repent and turn back to the Lord their God.

The combined impact of John's testimony to Jesus and Jesus' own dramatic announcement establishes that the great and terrible Day of the Lord, long-expected in the Old Testament, has now come. This electric announcement charges everything that follows in the Gospels. Those who behold Jesus repeatedly gasp in awestruck amazement, in recognition that the times of God are upon them. God himself is 'in' these times; he is present with his people. This is his 'special' time; Jesus is his 'Special Man'.

2   The coming, death and resurrection of God's Special Man, Jesus

The body of each Gospel, following its electrifying opening, demonstrates that Jesus is God's Special Man.

Each Gospel here narrates (1) Jesus' peremptory call of his disciples, (2) the dramatic power of his miracles of healing and deliverance of those oppressed with unclean spirits, (3) his amazing teaching of the crowds and (4) his irresistible power in the disputes with the religious establishment.

The Gospel-writers portray Jesus in a rapid succession of briefly narrated scenes. From his own lips Jesus reveals himself to be 'the Son of Man', God's Special Man who, according to Daniel 7, will judge the kingdoms of the world and then be given – by God – the never-ending rule over all peoples and nations, who will worship him.[4] Paradoxically, Jesus also reveals himself to be the humble Servant of the Lord prophesied in Isaiah 53, who, in obedience to God, will 'bear the sins of many'.

As Oscar Cullmann noted, Jesus thus fused within himself, as the Son of Man, 'the highest conceivable declaration of exaltation' and, as the Servant of the Lord, 'the expression of deepest humiliation'.[5]

Initially the disciples, like the general populace, probably followed Jesus in the belief that he was a prophet. Eventually, however, the Twelve came to conclude that he was the Lord's Anointed, his Messiah, raised up to deliver his people from their oppression by the Romans.

Jesus accepted this recognition as Messiah, but radically re-defined it. On one hand he raised Messiah to unimagined heights while on the other he lowered him to unexpected depths. As Son of Man, his role was infinitely higher than the Jews had ascribed to Messiah. As Suffering Servant of the Lord, he portrayed himself as subject to abject humiliation and rejection, a role which the Twelve found bewildering and utterly unacceptable. Instead of being bloodstained in victory he was to be bloodied in defeat. Humiliated, he was to suffer for the sins of his people.

Surprising as was Jesus' revelation of himself as Son of Man and Servant of the Lord, there was something infinitely more astonishing. In his own relationship with God, Jesus actually re-defined the inner character of God. By what Jesus taught about God and by his own prayer to God Jesus revealed him to be *Abba*, 'Father'. This word *Abba* is the everyday Aramaic for the small child's first articulation of the name of his male parent. For mother it is *Imma;* for father it is *Abba*. It is this word that Jesus uses – and teaches his disciples to use – for Yahweh, the God of Israel.

4   Daniel 7:13–14.
5   *The Christology of the New Testament* (London, SCM, 1955), 161.

Equally radical is Jesus' disclosure that he is himself, '*the* Son' of the God who is his Father, his *Abba*. Moreover, this is an exclusive relationship. 'No one knows the Son *except* the Father and no one knows the Father *except* the Son.'[6]

The Pharisees understood well Jesus' claims. 'This was why the Jews sought all the more to kill him, because he...called God his own Father, making himself equal with God.'[7] By calling God his *own* Father, Jesus was making himself equal with God.

At the heart of Jesus' relationship with the Twelve, therefore, was his re-definition of God as 'the Father' and his revelation to them that he, Jesus, was 'the Son'. Thus Jesus re-shaped the way these Jews thought about and related to God. He also taught them to pray, 'Our Father, in heaven...'

Jesus reveals the hitherto undreamed of secret, that at the heart of the universe[8] lies the relationship between God and Jesus, his Son, and the possibility of a relationship between God and all who belong to Jesus, his adopted sons and daughters.

Thus the body of the Gospel, by its rapid succession of cameos, reveals that Jesus is, indeed, God's 'Special Man' – his Messiah, defined as Son of Man and Servant of the Lord, and as the Son of the 'dear Father' – sent to Israel and to the world at this, God's 'Special Time'.

This body of the Gospel is not removed from history or geography. The names of the places where events took place are frequently given. Likewise, the ominous figure of Herod Antipas, tetrarch of Galilee-Peraea, lurks in the backdrop of all that Jesus does. When Jesus travels south to Jerusalem and Judaea he enters the realm of the Temple hierarchy and of Pontius Pilate. The names of disciples and of various individuals are given. Clearly the central section of the

---

6   Matthew 11:27; cf. Mark 8:38; 13:32; 14:36.
7   John 5:18.
8   A phrase suggested by the title of P.F. Jensen's book, *At the Heart of the Universe* (Homebush West, Lancer, 1991).

Gospel, like its beginning and end, is tied into time and space reality.

3   He will return, bringing history to its appointed end

The latter half of each Gospel is devoted to Jesus' movement to and arrival in Jerusalem. Here the historical information is concentrated. Places, times and people come before us in considerable detail.

During this final phase of the Gospel, Jesus teaches his disciples about the future. En route to Jerusalem he teaches them about his imminent rejection and death at the hands of the Temple authorities followed by his resurrection after three days.

Once in Jerusalem he teaches the Twelve about the period after he is no longer with them. He teaches about the coming of the Holy Spirit and that the Gospel will be carried to the nations with consequent persecution of his people. He foretells the destruction of the Temple and, beyond that, of the celestial coming of the Son of Man.

The Gospels reach their climax with the betrayal and arrest of Jesus on the Thursday evening. This is followed first by interrogation by the Jewish hierarchy, then, in the early morning of Friday, by the Roman prefect's examination of the accused and his determination that Jesus be handed over for crucifixion. The Roman soldiers lead Jesus outside the walls of Jerusalem and crucify him. By mid-afternoon he is dead.

The last part of the Gospels tell of the disciples' discovery on Sunday morning that Jesus' body is not in the tomb. The risen Lord then appears to the disciples on a number of occasions and then they see him no more.

The future belongs to God.

THE ORIGIN OF THE GOSPELS

How did these exciting accounts of the ministry and teaching of Jesus come to be written? The Gospels were written as the climax of the process of the pioneering phase in which the first churches were established. The sequence appears to have been:

AD 33	AD 40	AD 50	AD 60	AD 70
verbal gospelling	written collections	Letters	written Gospels	

Our working assumption then, with which most agree, is that the Gospels were written after the Letters, in fact, as the last part of the process.

What, then, is the origin of the written Gospels? Do the written Gospels arise out of the mission Letters? The answer must be No. It would not be possible to reconstruct even one story found in Mark from the Letters of Peter, to re-tell any story in Matthew from the Letter of James, to piece together any story in Luke from a letter of Paul or to re-create any story in John from the Letters of John. The Gospels were not manufactured out of the mission Letters.

Do the Gospels arise from pre-formed written sources? The answer is, 'Yes, in part'. The early collections of Jesus' teachings which were made available to the churches certainly appear to have been incorporated in the written Gospels:[9]

written sources → written Gospel

Yet such sources only appear to be components in the greater whole, of a total Gospel. They do not account for its overall shape.

Do the Gospels, then, arise from the mission preaching?

---

9   Not, however, in the Gospel of John where it is impossible to detect the underlying sources. This gospel has been called a 'seamless robe'.

The answer, so it seems, is Yes, at least in regard to the Gospel of Mark. The verbal message of Peter in Caesarea, as summarised in the Acts of the Apostles, bears a close similarity to the Gospel of Mark.[10] Peter's spoken Gospel appears to have given the shape to Mark's written Gospel:

Peter's spoken Gospel → Mark's written Gospel

If the the verbal outline of Peter's mission preaching became the 'skeleton', as it were, Peter's stories about Jesus were the flesh and sinews, which, with the skeleton, formed the Gospel of Mark as we have it. Mark's written Gospel is really an expanded version of Peter's spoken Gospel.

What, then is the relationship between Mark and the other three Gospels? Mark's Gospel was endorsed, but not embellished, by Matthew and Luke and incorporated into their Gospels. The Gospel of John, while not dependent on Mark's outline or specific content, nonetheless, broadly follows the same overall sequence.[11]

IS THE EVIDENCE IN THE GOSPELS ABOUT JESUS TRUE?

The answer is, 'Yes, the evidence in the Gospels is true and may be relied on as a basis for Christian faith'. Our grounds for such confidence are several:

First, the Gospels were written within living contact with Jesus – whether direct or at one remove – guaranteeing the truthfulness of the record. They were not produced in

---

10 See Acts 10:36–43.
11 Both the Markan and the Johannine chronology have in common this sequence:
      1. John's baptism of Jesus.
      2. Jesus' ministry in Galilee commences after John's arrest.
      3. Jesus' feeding of the 5000 at Passover time.
      4. Jesus' final journey from Galilee to Judaea.
      5. Jesus' arrest and execution at Passover in Jerusalem.

remoteness in time from Jesus, but are relatively close, flowing out of living contact with him, in the knowledge that many were alive who could, if necessary, contradict the details.

Second, there are multiple Gospels – four, in fact. We are not dependent on one witness but on four Gospels, arising out of four quasi-independent mission teams. A basic principle of evidence acceptable in a court of law is in place, namely, we have not one, but two or more witnesses. In fact, we have four witnesses.

Third, the stories about Jesus which comprise the written Gospel are uninventable. Had the Gospel writers sought to 'invent' a Jesus acceptable to the church and the world at the time of writing, they would scarely have written about a man of dubious parentage, a lowly tradesman from unheard-of Nazareth in obscure Galilee who finished his life disgraced on a Roman cross for treason against the Emperor. The improbability of the details supports their veracity.

Fourth, there are several points at which we can cross check the Gospels. Tacitus, the Roman historian confirms the details about the execution of 'Christus' at the hands of the Roman governor, Pontius Pilate. Matthew and Luke use the text of Mark's Gospel in their own Gospels but without embellishing or exalting Jesus beyond what Mark has written. At many points it is possible to crosscheck Matthew and Luke. But these writers are revealed to be sober and disciplined. If they prove to be reliable at those points when we can compare them with Mark we are confident that they are careful at other points.

Fifth, the Gospel-writers each tell their Jesus-story in a simple, matter-of-fact, even understated way, with a minimum of editorial comment. The facts about Jesus are allowed to speak for themselves. Although he is worshipped as the heavenly Lord of the world and of the church, the Gospels allow the readers to see Jesus in his thorough humanity. He comes before us as weary, thirsty and hungry. He is daunted by the prospect of the suffering that lies before him. We see him now moved with compassion, now with righteous anger. We observe him betrayed by a friend, abandoned by the rest of his disciples and degraded by his enemies. Painful reality is evident on every page of the Gospels.

Even apart from a belief in their divine inspiration, which this author holds, the Gospels prove themselves to be authentic records of Jesus' words and actions. We are able to say with confidence that the Gospels are a historically true record of the ministry and teaching of Jesus, God's Special Man.

QUESTIONS FOR REFLECTION AND DISCUSSION:

1. What are the main elements about Jesus which the Letters and the Gospels affirm?

2. How does Jesus define his role as God's Special Man in this, God's special time?

3. How does Jesus re-define the character of the covenant God of Israel?

FURTHER READING:

P.W. Barnett, *The Two Faces of Jesus* (Sydney, Hodder & Stoughton, 1990).

S. Kim, *The Son of Man as The Son of God* (Grand Rapids, Eerdmans, 1985).

I.H. Marshall, *The Origins of Christology* (Leicester, IVP, 1977).

Chapter Six

Truth about the Christmas Story

Many today, including bishops of the Church, have expressed scepticism about the historicity of the cluster of stories surrounding the birth of Jesus. It is fashionable to dismiss these stories as 'myth' while purporting to accept the deep meaning said to be implicit in them. It has become as predictable as Christmas itself that the media will at that time report the deep reservations felt about it by noted academics or churchmen.

PRELIMINARY QUESTIONS

Two important questions are: (1) Does the Bible actually say what is commonly believed about the Christmas Story? (2) Do the Bible writers intend their account to be taken as historically based or as edifying 'myth'?

Reflected in the scenes depicted on Christmas cards, children's nativity tableaus and straw-surrounded models of Mary, Joseph and baby Jesus in the stable, is a pictorial 'culture' of the Christmas Story. But on investigation much of what is believed to be in the Bible proves to be pure religious imagination. For example, the Gospels do not say that the manger was inside a covered building or that there were cattle nearby. The so-called 'wise men' – the *magi* – were probably Mesopotamian astrologers, but there is no mention that there were three of them.

It is important, therefore, that those who tend to dismiss

the Christmas Story as 'myth', first address the actual text of the Bible.

The fundamental question must be: did the original writers intend their narrative to be treated as historically based or as stories which may or may not be true but which, regardless of their factuality, have an edifying meaning. Straightforward reading of the texts of Matthew and Luke, the only two Gospel-writers who record these events, suggests that their accounts are to be taken at face value. Matthew and Luke wrote their stories as true narrative, the first part of the narrative of their Gospels. There is no justification for their early chapters to be regarded as unhistorical.

This must mean that for the birth stories to be regarded as 'myth', modern readers must arbitrarily go against the apparent intention of the original authors. In this case it must be asked what right do such readers have to derive *any* meaning from the text. It has become a mere piece of plasticine in their hands.

AGREEMENT AMID DIFFERENCE

It would be helpful for the reader of Matthew and Luke to recognise that these authors have not written 'straight history'. Each tells his story as he sees it. Each places the emphasis where he wills.

Matthew places his spotlight on *Joseph*. It is Joseph whom the angel of the Lord addresses. Joseph's dilemma with Mary's pre-marital pregnancy is commented on, but he, nonetheless, obediently marries her. Joseph it is who names the child, takes mother and child to and from Egypt, settling finally in Nazareth. According to Matthew, Joseph is an obedient man, loving to his pregnant betrothed and able to be guided by God, now here, now there. Mary, however, remains passive, silent throughout.

Matthew portrays Jesus as having been pre-figured by

Israel, God's historic people. Jesus' exodus from Egypt was that he might fulfil the prophecy, 'Out of Israel I have called my son'.[1] God's true 'son' is now here, a fact which his obedience through temptation will soon demonstrate. Matthew's facts are set within this theological matrix.

Luke, for his part, focuses all attention on *Mary.* According to Luke it is Mary who has the dilemma. How can she, an unmarried woman, bear 'the Son of the Most High'? In Luke's account it is Mary who emerges as faithful and obedient to God, a model of one who is poor and lowly whom the Lord will uplift. Joseph is silent and inactive throughout.

Luke is concerned to show that the birth of Jesus was in fulfilment of the holy prophets for the salvation of God's people, but also for the light of God to come to the Gentiles. Luke's facts are set within this matrix.

Matthew and Luke tell their stories with attention drawn to different parents, one to Joseph, the other to Mary. Each allows the great fulfilment motif to emerge, though in differing ways. For Matthew Jesus *is himself* Israel, God's true 'Son', whereas for Luke Jesus fulfils *the words* spoken by the prophets to Israel.

There are other differences. In Matthew's Gospel, Joseph and Mary appear to be living in Judaea at the time of the birth; in Luke they travel from Nazareth to Bethlehem in Judaea. Each writer has his key players in his story, Matthew the jealous Herod and the magi, Luke the aged Simeon and the prophetess Anna. Matthew's genealogy begins with Abraham and ends with Jesus; Luke reverses the chronology, beginning with Jesus and ending with Adam. These and other differences show that Matthew and Luke were not dependent on each other.

Nonetheless, despite the differences of historical detail and

---

1   Hosea 11:1.

theological emphasis these writers agree as to the core facts which comprise the Christmas Story:

1   Joseph belonged to the royal line of David, from whom the Messiah would come. Jesus did not become, but was '*born,* king of the Jews'.[2]
2   Jesus was not the biological son of Joseph. In his genealogy Matthew says that Joseph was the 'husband of Mary', not Jesus' father. Luke notes that Jesus was the son, 'so it was thought of Joseph'.[3] Powerful reality lies behind this subtle statement.
3   Mary's pregnancy occurred through the direct intervention of God during the period of her betrothal to Joseph.
4   The birth of Jesus, Mary's son, occurred at Bethlehem.
5   Herod was at that time king of Israel.

These points of agreement in writings which were written independently are impressive. If two witnesses to an accident tell their stories differently and with their own details but with agreement on the core facts the court would concur in their witness.

HOW COULD THE MESSIAH BE BORN OF A VIRGIN?

A problem for historicity is seen in the apparent hopeless contradiction between points (1) and (2) above. How could Jesus be the Messiah, 'born King of the Jews' as a descendant of David, if Joseph was not Jesus' biological father? The intervention of God in his conception broke Jesus' physical descent from David, from whom Messiah was to come.

---

2   Matthew 2:2.
3   Matthew 1:16; Luke 3:23.

The resolution of that problem is that paternity was not then, as it is now, seen to be dependent on biological process. Procreation was a mere means of birth; the name one bore was all-important.

In the culture of the Romans it was the family name, not blood relationship, that mattered. An adopted son might know and have a relationship with his biological father. But the man whose name he bore was the important thing; that man was the recognised and legal father.

For their part the Jews recognised the Levirate Marriage, under which a deceased man's line could be established by the union of his brother with the deceased's widow. Their firstborn son was regarded as truly son of the deceased, although the biological offspring of another.[4] Joseph named, registered and presented in the Temple the newborn baby; Jesus was known in Galilee as 'son of Joseph from Nazareth'.[5]

Because Jesus was known to be, and legally was, 'son of Joseph' he was indeed, through Joseph, a descendant of David, and thus qualified to be the Lord's Anointed, his Messiah. But equally, he was conceived by direct intervention of the Holy Spirit and was, on that account, according to Matthew, 'Emmanuel, God with us', and according to Luke the 'Son of God'.[6]

The virgin conception of Jesus was not on account of some scruple about sexuality. Some Christians of later years would come to regard sexual union as somehow unclean; but the culture of the Old Testament, under which Jesus was born and the Gospels were written, was entirely affirmative of sexual intercourse, that is, within the constraints of marriage. Rather, the virginal conception of Jesus marked him out as utterly different. He was truly a man; but he was uniquely the Son of God.

4   Leviticus 25:5–10.
5   Matthew 1:20–21; Luke 2:1–5; 3:22–24; John 1:42; 6:42.
6   Matthew 1:23; Luke 2:35; 3:22–23, 49; 4:3, 9.

'PROBLEMS' WITH THE BIRTH STORIES

Various problems have been raised with the Nativity Stories.

It is alleged that 'the rest of the New Testament is silent about the Nativity Stories'

It is often claimed that the rest of the New Testament 'knows nothing' of the birth stories recorded in Matthew and Luke. Particular store is made of the apparent silence of the Letters of Paul and the Gospel of Mark, the earliest Letters and Gospel respectively. Some then suggest that the birth stories are 'mythical' additions tacked on later to give Jesus credibility in the world of his time.

It is true that, with one exception, the mission Letters do not mention the circumstances of Jesus' birth. But then they say little about his historical life or ministry. These Letters make no mention of Mary or Joseph, nor, for that matter about Jesus as a teacher or worker of miracles. In fact, there are few details given in the Letters about his death and resurrection.

This 'silence' should not surprise us because, as we have noted earlier, the Letters were not the initial communication to the churches, which was by word of mouth. The Letters are for 'follow-up' purposes for those who had become Christians, to remind and to reinforce teachings which had already been received.

Again, as noted beforehand, such initial oral data was soon supplemented by written resources recounting phases of Jesus' ministry and his teachings. These were committed early to written form and circulated to many of the churches.[7] It is entirely reasonable to suppose that accounts of his birth were among these and that Matthew's and Luke's versions grew out of these. Thus there was no need

---

7   See Luke 1:1–2.

for the writers of the Letters to refer to circumstances of Jesus' birth: the recipients of the Letters were already informed.

The one exception is found in one of Paul's Letters. He writes to the Galatian churches:

> When the time had fully come,
> God sent his Son
> born of a woman,
> born under law,
> to redeem those [who were] under the law...[8]

This statement is gratuitously made. It is not introduced as new information, but as something well-established to make a point tangentially connected with it. Paul is discussing the need to be redeemed from the curse of the law of Moses, which was an issue at the time of writing, and it is in this regard that Paul introduces these words. Their solemn cadence implies that they are the well-rounded words of a creed or confession, not merely written *de novo* at that time by Paul nor, perhaps, heard for the first time by the Galatians. As such they are a perfect summary, in formal confessional terms, of the account which would come to comprise Luke's early chapters:

1   Luke's 'God has visited and redeemed his people...as he spoke by the mouths of his holy prophets'[9] corresponds with Paul's words, 'The time had fully come...to redeem'.
2   Luke's 'He...will be called Son of the Most High'[10] are closely related to Paul's 'God sent forth his Son'.
3   Luke's account of the angel's announcement to Mary of the supernatural conception of a son and his pointed

---

8   Galatians 4:4.
9   Luke 1:68–70.
10 Luke 1:32.

comment in the genealogy, eliminating the role of Joseph, (Jesus...the son of Joseph — so it was thought)[11] find a neat parallel in Paul's words, 'born of a woman'.

4 Luke's account of the parents' presentation of the child in the Temple and, later, their annual visit to Jerusalem for the Passover (included in which was the youthful Jesus' first Passover visit to Jerusalem) as 'according to [the] custom [of the Law]'[12] is quite in line with Paul's 'born under the law'.

In the light of these striking similarities of concept, though not of exact wording, it seems likely that Paul knew of the underlying tradition about Jesus' birth which will come to us in completed form in the early chapters of the Gospel of Luke. Historically, Paul's brief summary in a letter, written in all probability before AD 50, is an early witness to the circumstances of the birth of Jesus.

What, then, is to be said about the silence of the other Gospels, Mark and John?

Mark begins his Gospel with John the Baptist, who, however, is quickly off the scene to enable the writer dramatically to introduce the awesome figure of the Son of God. Mark has no genealogies, no birth stories, no details of the temptations; Jesus simply appears. In story after story Mark presents the irresistible power of Jesus to the amazement of the crowds and the bewilderment of the disciples. In his account everything points onwards to his death and resurrection in Jerusalem and beyond that to the destruction of the Temple and the return in glory of the Son of Man.

The omissions are striking. Mark recounts neither the birth story nor the resurrection story. Jesus merely appeared

---

11 Luke 1:26–38; 3:23.
12 Luke 3:27; 41.

and in like manner will, without warning, reappear. To say Mark knows nothing of the birth of Jesus or for that matter the resurrection of Jesus is to draw an inference from silence and one, moreover, which misses his presentation of the astonishingly mysterious character of the Son of Man who appears unannounced, who disappears, and who will reappear unannounced. An introduction giving birth and genealogy details would weaken the sense of immediacy which Mark seeks to establish from the very outset of his Gospel.

John sees Jesus as the life-laden Word of God through whom the cosmos had been made. He is that Word who became flesh and dwelt among the disciples, and so John is particularly concerned to recount the miracles of Jesus and Jesus' commentary on those miracles. These are the 'works' of Jesus which demonstrate that he is the Son of the Father who sent him. Whereas Mark presents Jesus as onwards-pointing, John's purpose is existential and relational. According to John, Jesus is the eternal Word and Son of God who, incarnate as Jesus, son of Joseph from Nazareth, reveals the invisible God, making possible relationship with God as Father. John begins by introducing Jesus' eternal being (his 'was'-ness); he was prior to the Creation and indeed was responsible for it. By omitting genealogy and birth story, John by-passes Jesus' relationship with Israel as the fulfilment of the prophets. Jesus simply appears as an adult at the time of the baptising activities of John the Baptist. As with Mark, for us to conclude that John knows nothing of the circumstances of Jesus' birth would be to draw an inference from silence and, as also in the case of Mark, to miss the theological intention of the author as expressed in his literary presentation. For John to have introduced genealogy or birth story would have caused the loss of the existential immediacy which is his clear purpose.

Indeed, in this regard it does appear that John does make reference to the virginal conception of Jesus, but obliquely. Describing Jesus' coming to his people John writes:

94

to all who received him...he gave the right to become children of God.

John then adds that these were

born
not of blood[s],
nor of the will of flesh,
nor of the will of a man [husband],
but of God.[13]

But this describes the manner of the virginal conception of Jesus. Jesus birth arose not from human passion nor a husband's decision; it was 'of God'. It appears that John has knowingly used the circumstances of the birth of Jesus, God's child, as a paradigm for the spiritual *re*-birth of the children of God. Moreover, John's lack of further comment suggests that his readers would nod their heads in understanding of the analogy he was making, so well known was the miraculous mode by which 'the word became flesh'.

Similarly, John knew that because Jesus was the Messiah he was the descendant of David who was to be born in Bethlehem.[14] It is a measure of the blindness of the Jews of Jerusalem to Jesus' identity as Messiah[15] that they are unaware of his Davidic descent or of his birth in Bethehem. To them Jesus is merely an enigmatic Galilean. But John knows these things, referring ironically to the Jews' ignorance of them. Clearly, John knows that Jesus, as Messiah, was descended from David and that he was born in Bethlehem.

So far from John not knowing the circumstances of Jesus' birth, it emerges from his Gospel that he knows the fundamental truths that, on the one hand Jesus was

---

13 John 1:12–13 (my translation).
14 John 1:41; 4:25; 7:42.
15 John 1:25; 7:26, 41; 10:24; 12:34.

supernaturally 'born of God' and that, on the other, he was the Messiah descended from David and born in Bethlehem. Not only does John know these things, but the manner in which he writes suggests that his readers know them, too, as opposed to the blind Jews of Jerusalem who could not penetrate the reality of Jesus' true identity.

In short, we reject the suggestion that the birth stories are of late composition, tacked on to the beginning of the Gospels. The literature of three of the four missions makes reference to the circumstances of Jesus' birth as represented by the writings of Matthew, Luke/Paul and John. The early reference in Paul's letter to the Galatians, so closely connected to Luke's presentation, establishes that it was indeed an early tradition in the churches. Only the mission Letters/Gospel of Peter/Mark are silent on this subject. But it would be precarious on the basis of Mark's silence to conclude that his mission leader, Peter, was unaware of these things. And, as we have seen, Mark's manner of presenting the claims of the Son of God was one of eschatological immediacy, which the introduction of genealogy or birth stories would have blunted.

It is alleged that 'Luke's account is at odds with secular history'

Luke states that Jesus was born in Bethlehem because his parents had to return to their ancestral city to be 'enrolled' and that this occurred when Quirinius was governor of Syria.[16] But, according to Josephus,[17] Quirinius' enrolment or Census-taking of the people is known to have occurred in AD 6, ten years after the death of Herod the Great. Earlier, Luke located the birth of John the Baptist in the time of Herod. Jesus' birth followed closely after the birth of John.[18]

---

16   Luke 2:1–7.
17   *Antiquities of the Jews* xviii.1.
18   Luke 1:5, 24, 26, 39.

Matthew is even clearer that Jesus was born some years before the death of Herod.[19] On the face of it Luke has made a mistake of considerable magnitude and, to that extent, he has considerably weakened the credibility of his narrative.

However, to claim that Luke has made this error raises major problems. (1) As noted above, Luke does locate the birth of Jesus in the time of Herod. Is he internally, as well as externally, mistaken? (2) In the next chapter Luke reveals pinpoint accuracy as to who was ruling the various parts of Herod's former realm at the time John began his ministry. Herod's realm was divided and the various rulers appointed in 4 BC, ten years before the Census marking the annexation of Judaea.[20] If Luke knows about the division of Herod's kingdom, surely he would know about the Census for the annexation of Judaea as a province ten years later. It was a famous event which sparked off the uprising led by Judas the Galilean; Luke himself calls it 'the Census'.[21] (3) Likewise, why would Luke have Galilean taxpayers, under the jurisdiction of Herod Antipas, tetrarch of Galilee, coming to Judaea to be enrolled for Roman taxes that they did not have to pay? As Galileans Joseph and Mary paid taxes to Herod Antipas, not to the Roman governor of Judaea.

But there is another explanation, which solves the problem. The critical verse – Luke 2:2 – is brief, a mere eight words in the original Greek:

This was the first enrolment when Quirinius was governor of Syria.[22]

Critical to this sentence is the word, 'first'. The Greek word *(prōtos)* often means 'former', as in the opening words of

---

19 Matthew 2:16.
20 Luke 3:1–2.
21 Acts 5:37
22 The Revised Standard Version.

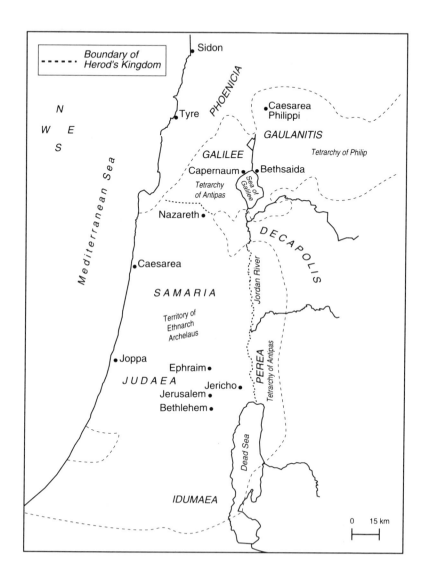

Map 4: *Herod's kingdom divided*

Luke's second volume, the Acts of the Apostles ('the former book'). Understood in this way Luke 2:2 could be understood to mean:

> This was a former enrolment *before* Quirinius was governor of Syria.

In other words, Luke knows about the famous enrolment under Quirinius in AD 6, but the enrolment of Luke 2:2, during which Jesus was born, was an earlier, relatively unknown enrolment which would have occurred during the latter years of Herod the Great. Indeed, 'first' meaning 'former' or 'earlier' makes good sense; we do not know of enrolments after Quirinius' enrolment.

To what, then, is Luke referring? Frankly, we do not have evidence of an enrolment for tax purposes during Herod's reign. However, we know of an oath taking to the Emperor Augustus in 7 BC in which all Jews were obliged to participate.[23] It was controversial at the time: the Pharisees refused to give the oath. Perhaps it was for this that Joseph and Mary journeyed to Bethlehem. Certainly, this is conjectural; but it is by no means impossible.

It is alleged that 'the Birth Stories are mythological'

In the world of Matthew and Luke it was not uncommon for biographies of great men, past and present, to be written. These sometimes described in terms that we recognise as mythological, the circumstances of the birth and boyhood of such notables, for example, the philophers Plato and Pythagoras and the soldiers/statesmen Alexander the Great and Augustus.[24]

Plato (427–347 BC), the philosopher of Athens, was the

---

23 *Antiquities of the Jews* xvii.42.
24 See D.R. Cartlidge and D.L. Dungan, *Documents for the Study of the Gospels* (Philadelphia, Fortress Press, 1980), 129–136.

Coin featuring head of Alexander the Great

son of Ariston and Periktione. Ariston, unable to achieve the pregnancy of his wife, saw a vision of Apollo. Abstaining from further sexual intercourse, Periktione brought forth a child from Apollo.[25]

Pythagoras (6th century BC), a philosopher from Samos, was said to be a descendant of Zeus. But some said he was begotten by Apollo.[26]

The Macedonian king Alexander the Great (356–323 BC) conquered the Orient. A fiery vision granted to Alexander's parents Philip and Olympias before their marriage suggested that their son would be the descendant of the god Heracles.[27]

Like Plato, it was believed that Augustus (63 BC–AD 14), the Princeps of Rome in whose time Jesus was born, was the son of Apollo. As his mother slept in the

---

25 Diogenes Laertius, *Lives of Eminent Philosophers* 3.1–2, 45. Diogenes Laertius wrote in the third century AD, about seven centuries after Plato, but claims dependence on sources contemporary with Plato.
26 Iamblichus, *The Life of Pythagoras* 3–10.
27 Plutarch, *Parallel Lives, Alexander* 2.1–3.2.

Temple of Apollo a serpent entered her body and she was impregnated with the seed of Apollo.[28]

These biographies illustrate the widespread belief that great philosophers, conquerors and statesmen were not mere mortals, but owed their greatness as heroes to the gods from whom they were descended.

Are we to bracket the birth stories of Matthew and Luke with those of these great men of the Graeco-Roman world? Are the stories of Jesus 'mythological'?

1   There can be little doubt that Matthew and Luke have written their stories carefully, with particular readerships in mind. But they are not written in a Gentile format, along mythological lines. Luke has carefully modelled his stories about the births of John the Baptist and Jesus on Old Testament stories associated with Samson and Samuel.[29] The literary influences on Matthew are uncertain, except that they, too, appear to be Jewish in this the most Jewish of the Gospels. It is highly unlikely that Matthew or Luke, writing out of the Jewish tradition, would have known, let alone used, either the form or the content of Gentile stories in which heroes were descended from the gods. For Jews and Christians idolatry and its associated mythology were utterly abhorrent, matters for thorough repentance.

2   Gentile Christians of the next century – the apologist Justin, for example – who were surrounded by the gods of Graeco-Roman mythology, were rock solid in their commitment to the factuality of the birth stories. Unlike us who live in western secular culture and who are relatively unacquainted with idolatry and mythology, the converted Gentile of that era knew the difference between the history of the Gospel and the mythology of gods and heroes. They had good reason to be sure in

---

28   Suetonius, *Lives of the Caesars* II.94.1–7.
29   Luke 1:5–7; Judges 13:2–5; Luke 1:46–55; 1 Samuel 2:1–10.

their own minds about these things. Justin understood that the abandonment of idolatry and mythology in favour of the confession of Christ could cost him his life.[30] In Justin's case it did; he is known as Justin *Martyr*.

3   The Gospel accounts are written in a historical, as opposed to a mythological, style. The stories of gods and heroes are usually told in utterly improbable ways. For example, snakes are involved in the gods' impregnation of the mothers of Alexander the Great and Augustus. There is a minimum of specific detail of person, time or place. The whole has the air of improbability. Neither the writer nor the reader expects what is written to be taken literally, quite the reverse in fact. The mythological stories are meant to recognise the special character of famous people, not to be taken as history. By contrast Matthew and Luke recount their narratives soberly and with a significant emphasis on the specifics of history and on the historical context of the event:

a. Matthew and Luke place the birth within the reign of Herod, Luke adding the significant detail that an imperial decree of Augustus requiring the registration of people brought Joseph to his ancestral town, Bethlehem.[31]

b. Matthew's description of Herod's paranoia about the one born to be king as sought by the *Magi* is on a par with the king's evil reputation. A contemporary work says of Herod: 'He shall cut off their chief men with the sword, and destroy them in secret places, so that no one may know where their bodies are. He shall slay the old and the young, and he shall not spare.'[32] Four centuries later reference would still be made to Herod's cruelty to children, including his own offspring.[33] This is reflected in Augustus' grim joke

---

30   *First Apology* xx–xxv.
31   Luke 2:1–5.
32   *Assumption of Moses* 6.
33   Macrobius, *Saturnalia*, tr. P. Davis, (New York, Columbia University Press, 1969), 171.

that he would rather be Herod's pig than Herod's son. To the pseudo-Jew Herod, the pig was safe since its meat was forbidden to Jews. But his sons were not; he killed three of them! The slaughter of the boys of Bethlehem is quite consistent with Herod's well-documented character.

c. The so-called 'wise men from the east', so easily dispensed with as legendary, are referred to by the word *magi,* from which our word magician is derived.[34] These *magi* were probably astrologers from Mesopotamia where there was intense study of the heavens.

d. Even the appearances of the bright lights seen by the shepherds or the star which the magi saw and followed may have been associated with the conjunction of Jupiter and Saturn which occurs every 805 years, but which occurred three times in AD 7. In AD 6 Jupiter and Saturn were joined by Mars forming a brilliant triangle.[35] It is quite believable that, having seen the astonishing happenings in the heavens, the *magi* should journey to Israel. For centuries it had been believed that a world ruler would arise in the east and that his coming would be heralded by a star.[36]

e. God's guidance of Joseph by dreams and of Mary by angels are not part of our experience in the secular society. But if we believe in God then he may guide his servants by whatever means he chooses. Dreams continue to play a very important place in many cultures. Things unusual to people living in western societies should not be rejected on grounds of unfamiliarity.

---

34 Bar-Jesus, also known as Elymas, who was associated with Sergius Paulus, Proconsul of Cyprus, was a *magos,* a sorcerer. (Acts 13:6, 8).

35 *Time* Magazine, 27 December, 1976, 27.

36 See e.g. Tacitus, *Histories* 5:13: '...the ancient scriptures of their priests [i.e. the Jews] alluded to...the time...when the Orient would triumph and from Judaea would go forth men destined to rule the world'.

While the accounts of Matthew and Luke are cast in a theological form, as befitting the coming of the Messiah – Emmanuel, that is, 'God with us' – there is no rational reason to reject the essentially historical nature of the stories about the birth of Jesus. The various objections to the historical basis of the Nativity Stories – that they find no echo outside those two Gospels, that Luke's account is at odds with Josephus and that the stories are mythological – are able to be answered.

As with the Gospels generally the Nativity Stories are not told as mundane history. There is an emotional and inspirational element to these stories, what we might call theological poetry. This is history intended to move the spirit within us to worship and thank God for his great gift to us, the child who was born king of the Jews, who as the mature Jesus would become the Saviour of us all.

QUESTIONS FOR REFLECTION AND DISCUSSION:

1. Is it a problem for us that Matthew and Luke narrate the Nativity Stories with differing theological emphases and with details peculiar to each?

2. How might we account for the silence of Mark and John with regard to the birth of Jesus?

3. Do you think Matthew and Luke are relating 'myth' when they relate the stories of Jesus' birth?

FURTHER READING:

P.W. Barnett, *Is the New Testament History?* (Sydney, Hodder & Stoughton, 1986).

P.L. Maier, *First Christmas* (London, Mowbrays, 1971).

R.T. France, 'Scripture, Tradition and History in the Infancy Narratives of Matthew', in D. Wenham, *Gospel Perspectives* Vol. 1 (Sheffield, JSOT, 1980), 239–257.

Chapter Seven

Truth about the deity of Jesus

In this chapter and the one following we face the two most critical questions about Jesus: (1) Is he the Son of God? (2) Did he rise from the dead? If the answer to either question is No, then Christians should abandon their faith and immediately discontinue any attempt to persuade others to accept it. The Christian faith would be without any basis in reality. But, on the other hand, if Jesus is the Son of God who did rise to life from the dead then he has the claim to exercise the Lordship of God over all people everywhere.

Much is at stake, therefore, for both the Christian and the non-Christian, in the answers to those questions.

THE RE-DEFINITION OF GOD: THE EVIDENCE OF THE MISSION LETTERS

The four mission leaders – James, Peter, John and Paul – were Jews. James' Jewishness is quite apparent in his letter. Peter and John, as apostles in the early church, continued to attend the Temple at the set hours of prayer; Peter scrupulously observed Jewish food laws and avoided table fellowship with Gentiles.[1] Paul had been a leading younger scholar and activist in the sect of the Pharisees, who were devoted to the ideological and ritual purity of Israel.[2] He did not abandon the practices of Judaism after his conversion.

---

1   Acts 3:1; 10:14, 28.
2   Galatians 1:13–14.

For example, he placed himself under a Nazarite vow and sought to arrive in Jerusalem in time for the great festivals.[3]

These men were devoted to Yahweh, the covenant God of Israel. They were brought up to confess, day by day, that Yahweh their God, was One, and that they loved him with all their heart. Yet, as we read their mission Letters, we are astonished by the way they now refer to God. Each mission leader writes of 'God *and* the Lord Jesus Christ', or 'God the Father *and* the Lord Jesus Christ', or 'the Father *and*…his Son Jesus Christ'.[4]

As Jews these men would die rather than blaspheme the name of Yahweh their God. Yet they now call God *Father,* write *and* next to his name and add the name of the *Lord Jesus Christ.* They have re-defined the God who is 'One' as two persons, in some cases adding also the Holy Spirit.[5] How can this be?

Yahweh as 'One' means that He is unique and incomparable so far as other gods are concerned. However, Yahweh's Oneness says nothing about His *inner* character. In the Old Testament the many references to God achieving his purposes by His Word or Wisdom suggest that these attributes are personal and share in the deity of Yahweh,[6] thus preparing the way for the revelation of God's inner character as Father, Son and Spirit.

The references given above to God and Jesus are (1) *gratuitous* – they reinforce but do not set out to establish an attitude towards God as now re-defined; (2) *independent* – the mission Letters are written to separate clusters of congregations; and (3) *early* – within two decades of Jesus. That this re-definition of God occurred so close to Jesus' ministry must be regarded as historically secure.

---

3   Acts 18:18.
4   James 1:1; 2 Peter 1:3; 1 Thessalonians 1:2; 1 John 1:3; cf. 2 John 3.
5   1 Peter 1:2; 1 John 4:2; Galatians 4:4–6; 2 Thessalonians 2:13; 1 Corinthians 12:4–6; 2 Corinthians 13:14.
6   See L.W. Hurtado, *One God One Lord* (Fortress Press, Philadelphia, 1988).

How is it that these Jews have come to re-define Yahweh, their covenant God? Clearly it is the opinion they have come to that Jesus is the Son of God and *the Lord* which has led them to bracket his name with God and to regard God as the *Father* of Jesus, his Son. Fundamental to this, however, is their conviction that they have not abandoned the faith of their fathers. Jesus is the fulfilment of God's covenant with Israel, the true goal which had always been in sight.

HOW DID THESE JEWISH MEN COME TO THIS OPINION?

Undoubtedly it had been the impact of Jesus on them which caused them to think of him as *the Son of God* and *the Lord* and, as a result, to re-define God. In our opinion there can be no reasonable doubt that both of these terms go back to Jesus himself.

Let us note Paul's words in a letter written in the late forties, that is a mere decade and a half after Jesus. He appeals to the common experience of the Spirit of God as a result of which he and his readers cry, '*Abba,* Father'.[7] Paul's Galatian readers were Greek-speaking; they would not have known the Aramaic word *Abba* – Paul had introduced them to this word. Jews did not speak about or to God by such a familiar domestic term. But Jesus used this word to address God, as we know from Mark's account of Jesus' prayer in the Garden of Gethsemane just before his arrest.[8] Based on Jesus' practice and example the word *Abba* would have come into currency among the early Christians in Jerusalem and through them to Paul.

But the word *Abba* goes back to Jesus. If God is *Abba,* Father, then Jesus is the Son. With its use Jesus re-defined

---

7   Galatians 4:6; cf. Romans 8:15.
8   Mark 14:36.

the covenant God of Israel. The mission leaders almost certainly must have derived this redefinition from Jesus.

Another Aramaic word embedded in Paul's Greek Letters is *Mara,* Lord. The words *Maran atha* mean, 'Come, Lord'. Here is the prayer of the original Aramaic-speaking disciples calling out to the risen Jesus to return to them. But this too, almost as certainly, goes back to Jesus. During the disputes of the final week, Jesus identified himself as David's son who was also David's Lord, his *Mara.*[9]

The critical terms the Son of God and the Lord, which are commonly used of Jesus in the Greek Letters of the mission leaders, can be shown to rest on Aramaic originals *Abba* and *Mara* which, almost certainly, derive from Jesus himself. It is Jesus who, by his use of such terms, has re-defined the covenant God of Israel.

JESUS ACCORDING TO THE MISSION GOSPELS

The Gospels are narratives from which readers must draw their conclusions

Broadly speaking, the Gospels are biographies about Jesus. A Gospel is not a dogmatic treatise about him, as was, for example, Athanasius' *Incarnation of the Word,* written in the fourth century, which presents a systematically worked-out view of Jesus ready for the reader to adopt.

The Gospels, however, consist of many brief episodes focused on Jesus set within a narrative framework. The Gospels let the reader see and hear the living person, Jesus. The Gospel writers want the reader to reach the conclusions about Jesus which they have reached. But the readers are left free to do this based on their own reactions to Jesus. Significant reflection on the part of the readers is implied.

---

9   Mark 12:35–37.

They are not handed a theological formula on a plate and told to swallow it.

Jesus: God's Special Man for God's Special Time

Jesus reveals his sense of God-given *urgency*. This is now God's special moment and Jesus is God's special man. Repeatedly he says that he is *sent,* that he *must* do this or that;[10] he is under divine constraint. Jesus is immensely purposeful, not to do more of the same but to do something new. Repeatedly he says, 'I *came* not to do...but...' (e.g. 'I came not to call the righteous, but sinners').

Jesus is the Heaven-sent agent of God, come to accomplish God's will for his people at this, the end-time. Jesus announces and then will establish the dynamic rule of God in the world. In this regard Jesus constantly refers to himself as *the Son of Man,* the human figure who is God's appointee to exercise God's dominion over all peoples and whom all peoples will *worship.*[11]

Jesus, as this *Son of Man,* is a divine figure. Yet his deity is not free-standing, but dependent on God. He exercises the divine functions of forgiving others their sins and of judging the human race on the last day, but only as authorised to do so by God.[12] Jesus does all things under and by the *authority* of God, as *sent* by God. He is obedient to the will of God, but at terrible cost to himself.

Jesus is *God* in the sense that, as his *Son,* he perfectly represents the *Father* to us. The Son reveals God as he represents him; but he does not replace him. The Son's deity is inseparable from his obedience to God.

Those who look for Bible passages where Jesus says, in as many words, 'I am God', will look in vain. Jesus is, indeed, 'God' but in the Bible's own terms, not ours.

---

10 e.g. Mark 8:31; Luke 24:44.
11 Daniel 7:14; cf. Matthew 28:17.
12 Mark 2:10; John 5:27.

Jesus speaks in Parables, is a Parable

Jesus usually speaks in a parable. He communicates his message by a story or a figure of speech, drawing the hearers into his teaching by the artless telling of some real-life situation: 'A sower went out to sow...' But suddenly the hearers discover that they are part of the story: the story is really about each listener. He or she asks, 'Which soil am *I* into which his seed fell?'

When Jesus speaks about himself he uses the same indirectness. He speaks about himself as God, but it is allusively, even obliquely. His words are sharply spoken and call for sharp listening. Those present with him ask themselves, 'Who is this man?'

For Jews of the time, who knew their scriptures, Jesus' teaching about himself was provocative and unmistakable. He often spoke about himself in terms which echoed Yahweh's teaching about himself found in the Old Testament. Jesus' words would not 'pass away'; Yahweh's words would 'stand forever'.[13] Jesus said he was the 'bridegroom...with' the people; but Yahweh was the bridegroom of Israel.[14] Jesus often spoke of himself as the shepherd, searching, caring and giving himself for the lost sheep; but Yahweh was the good shepherd of Israel.[15] Jesus said that his words were the rock on which to build; Yahweh was the rock of safety for his covenant people.[16]

Jesus' most assertive identification of himself with the God of Israel – who identified himself to Moses as 'I am' – is to be heard in his 'I am' sayings, which are to be found represented independently across the Gospel traditions of John and Mark.[17]

---

13 Matthew 24:35; Isaiah 40:8.
14 Mark 2:19; Isaiah 62:5.
15 Mark 14:27; Luke 15:3–7; John 10:11–16; Psalm 23:1; Ezekiel 34:15.
16 Matthew 7:24–27; Isaiah 28:16.
17 See e.g. John 8:58; 18:6; Mark 13:6.

Three times in John chapter 8 Jesus claims to be 'I am':

> You will die in your sins unless you believe that *I am* (v.24).

> When you have lifted up the Son of Man, then you will know that *I am* (v.28).

> Before Abraham was, *I am* (v.58).

But *I am* was the name by which Yahweh, the God of Israel, revealed himself to Moses.[18]

In Mark's account Jesus predicts that false messiahs will arise, claiming in Jesus' name, to be 'I am'.[19] So fundamental was Jesus' self-description as *I am* that those who seek to imitate him will take the same words. Again, when the High Priests ask Jesus, 'Are you the Christ, the Son of the blessed?' Jesus replies, '*I am* and you shall see the Son of Man seated at the right hand of power, and coming with the clouds of heaven'.[20] At this the Temple hierarchy accused him of blasphemy.

In short, Jesus spoke about himself as 'God', but in allusive and indirect terms, which, nonetheless, were unmistakable in their intent to those who were alert listeners. But Jesus does not replace God. As the obedient Son, he unveils the unimaginable inner relationships of Father, Son and Spirit, previously unrevealed within the persona of Yahweh, who is 'One'.

THE GOSPEL WRITERS AND THEIR READERS

The Gospel writers seek to draw their readers into a relationship with Jesus in terms of his true identity as deity, as the divine Son of God. How do they do this?

---

18 Exodus 3:14.
19 Mark 13:6.
20 Mark 14:62–63.

Although each writer has his own distinctive style and emphasis, two features are in common:

First, each writer says something arresting about Jesus at or near the beginning of his Gospel. Matthew introduces Jesus as 'the son of David...the Christ', Mark as 'the Son of God' and Luke and John as 'the Word'. The reader is immediately alerted to Jesus as a very important person, and to the need to pay careful attention to that person as the Gospel unfolds.

Second, the writers having focused attention on Jesus in the numerous episodes that follow the introductions, reach a critical point when someone recognises and confesses Jesus' true identity. In Matthew Peter confesses Jesus to be 'the Christ', in Mark the centurion confesses Jesus to be 'the Son of God' and in John, Thomas addresses Jesus as 'my Lord and my God'.[21]

The writer positions me alongside the confessor and invites me to say the same words to Jesus.

The Gospel writers have reached radical and profound conclusions about Jesus. They have taken the considerable trouble to write their Gospels so that I will share their conclusions about Jesus and so that I will relate to him in the same way they do. They want me, the reader, to address Jesus in terms of his true identity, as the One sent from God, the Son of God, who is to be worshipped.

---

21 Matthew 16:16; Mark 15:39; John 20:28.

QUESTIONS FOR REFLECTION AND DISCUSSION:

1. How do the Gospels re-define God, and why?

2. Is Jesus God? If so, in what sense?

3. Discuss the method used by the Gospel writers to encourage us to accept their view of Jesus.

FURTHER READING:

P.W. Barnett, *The Two Faces of Jesus* (Sydney, Hodder & Stoughton, 1990).

M. J. Harris, *Jesus as God* (Grand Rapids, Baker, 1992).

Chapter Eight

Truth about the resurrection of Jesus

The heart of the apostles' message was the resurrection of Jesus. Whether it was Peter preaching to Jews in Jerusalem or Paul preaching to Gentiles in Athens their announcement focused on 'the resurrection' of Jesus from the dead.[1] The focal point of the New Testament and of Christianity is, in Paul's words, 'Jesus Christ, risen from the dead'.[2]

The apostle Paul, then, was quite correct when he said that

> if Christ has not been raised
> then our proclamation is in vain
> and your faith is in vain.
> We are [even] found to be misrepresenting God.[3]

Thus Christianity in a nutshell is (1) the *proclamation* by the apostles and (2) the *faith* of the church: *that Christ was raised from the dead.*[4]

But if God did not, as a matter of fact, raise Jesus from the dead then both proclamation and faith are vain, literally 'empty'. Worst of all, these apostles, who were Jewish men, had proved to be 'false witnesses' of the God of Israel. In short, if the resurrection did not take place, the message and faith of Christianity were utterly devoid of reality and those

---

1   Acts 4:33; 17:18.
2   2 Timothy 2:8.
3   1 Corinthians 15:14 (my translation).
4   cf. 1 Corinthians 15:11.

who proclaimed it were blasphemers of their covenant God.

Historically, the raising of Jesus caused his identity claims as the Son of God to be validated and his sayings and actions remembered. There were a number of 'messiahs' and 'prophets' in that general era, each of them with followers. But, in each case, their movements died with them; almost nothing of their deeds or words have survived.

Jesus, however, was survived by an ongoing movement which went from strength to strength and quickly outgrew the following which had arisen during his ministry period. It was the fact of the resurrection and the coming of the Spirit which gave the impetus for this rapid growth.

In the period immediately after Jesus, the movement was bursting with activity. The Old Testament was scoured for possible references to the Christ who was to come. Lists of prophecies seen to have been fulfilled in Jesus were compiled. Creeds and hymns focused on Jesus were written. A format to remember his death in the bread and the wine was created. His teaching was committed to memory and, in all probability, to written form.[5] Ministry among Jews was exploding, and in time, broke out of Jewish constraints in a number of semi-autonomous missions, including that of Philip to the Samaritans and Godfearers and Paul to the Gentiles. It is highly unlikely that this whirl of activity would have occurred apart from the resurrection of Jesus.

The resurrection is the eruption which set off the chain reaction within early Christianity: (1) in Jerusalem the collection of now-fulfilled prophecies, the establishing of credal and liturgical formulae, the writing of hymns to Jesus, (2) in Jerusalem and Judaea the mission work among Jews, (3) which rapidly spread to Samaria, Phoenicia, Cyprus, Syria, (4) and beyond that to Cilicia, Galatia, the provinces encircling the Aegean Sea and then westwards, to Italy and to Rome itself.

---

5   Luke 1:1.

It is apparent that the resurrection of Jesus from the dead is critical to Christianity. What evidence is there for the historical reality of the resurrection?

In giving this evidence, no assumptions should be made about the God-given origin, or otherwise, of the New Testament, except that the literature is as broadly historical as the 'secular' histories of the period. This is a reasonable assumption. The documents which comprise the New Testament are demonstrably as historical in character as, say, the writings of Josephus or Philo who are both Jews and who write within the timeframe in which the New Testament was written.

Many will not accept the God-dimension, that is, the possibility of miracles and of supernatural intervention in time and space. For them, philosophically speaking, the resurrection is impossible. Perhaps, though, as the reader considers the historical evidence for the resurrection, the philosophical structure of thought will be enlarged. If, based on evidence, the resurrection did happen, then one's mindset about what might or might not happen has to be, to that extent, modified.

As we stand in the shoes of the people of the first century we are confronted with a group of people who are convinced that their historical founder and leader has been raised from the dead.

Their follow-up literature in the Mission Letters assumes, but makes no effort to prove, the resurrection; so much is it taken to be beyond doubt. Key figures like James, Peter and Paul, who had nothing to do with one another before the First Easter, have each been profoundly, though differently, changed by the fact of the resurrection. Separate, but dovetailing, traditions relating to the resurrection on 'first day of the week' and the 'third day' after the crucifixion are in circulation, the one emanating from the Galilean women, the other from the twelve disciples. When the various accounts are compared the risen Jesus was seen and heard by between five and six hundred people over twelve known occasions during a forty-day period. The life and death zeal these Jews had for Yahweh and for his Temple and Sabbath is now expressed as life and death zeal for the risen Jesus, though the Sabbath is still observed and the Temple attended.

REFERENCES TO RESURRECTION IN THE LETTERS ARE INCIDENTAL

It is striking that the Letters of the mission leaders – James, Peter, John and Paul – never argue for the truth of the resurrection of Jesus. The writers assume that the readers accept its reality as now well-established and not in contention. However, while much of the information about the resurrection of Jesus is not part of the present argument in a Letter, it is introduced gratuitously, to support that argument.

This is not to say that the original hearers, whether they were Jews or Gentiles, would easily have accepted the resurrection of Jesus from the dead. Jews were looking for a universal resurrection at the *end* of history. The resurrection of an individual beforehand who was permanently, as opposed to temporarily, alive would have been a novelty. Gentiles of the Greek world believed in the immortality of the soul after the decay of the deceased. The resurrection of the body would have struck them as decidedly odd: some of Paul's hearers in Athens, when they heard of the resurrection of the dead, mocked the apostle.[6] Only powerful arguments from the apostles could have convinced Jews and Gentiles to become Christians; in particular, only powerful arguments would convince them that Jesus was actually raised from the dead.

---

6   Acts 17:32.

But the situation we encounter in the Letters is not one of argument. Although such references as there are to the resurrection are often made in passing, to reinforce some other aspect of Christian belief or behaviour, such references are frequent. To excise them would leave the New Testament an unreadable bundle of rags and tatters.

James and *John* do not make direct reference to the resurrection of Jesus. But they do speak of his second coming which, of course, is presupposed by his resurrection.[7] This indicates the degree to which both writers and readers took Jesus' resurrection to be an established fact.

Peter speaks of the resurrection of Jesus from the dead as the basis of the believers' faith and hope and of their forgiveness before God.[8] But it is not something for which Peter has to contend, but rather is given as a basis for godly confidence.

The gratuitous nature of resurrection references is splendidly illustrated by *Paul's* major reference to the resurrection of Jesus – 1 Corinthians 15:3–8. Paul is responding to a report that some of the Corinthians have expressed doubts about their own bodily resurrection. 'How can some of you say there is no resurrection of the dead?' he asks.[9]

Paul corrects this theological error by appealing to the uncontroversial fact of the death, the burial, the resurrection on the third day and the subsequent appearances of the risen Christ on a number of occasions. The Corinthians will be raised from the dead because Christ *has been* raised from the dead.[10] But the fact is not in doubt and does not have to be argued. He is reminding them of something which they

---

7   James 5:9; cf. 2:1; 5:15; 1 John 3:2.
8   1 Peter 1:3, 21; 3:18, 21.
9   1 Corinthians 15:12.
10 1 Corinthians 15:20–21.

already know as a basis of getting their thinking straight on this current issue.

We conclude that James, Peter, John and Paul – and with them Jude and the writer of Hebrews[11] – were convinced of the truth of the resurrection of Jesus. Where did this conviction originate? There is no special pleading, no propping up of their case. The most reasonable explanation for their convictions is that they arose from *fact,* the fact that Jesus was raised from the dead.

THE CHANGED LIVES OF JAMES, PETER AND PAUL

Three of those named as having seen the risen Christ – James, Peter and Paul[12] – died as martyrs three decades after the resurrection. James was executed in Jerusalem AD 62 at the hands of the High Priest Annas II, Peter and Paul in Rome in the mid-sixties by the Emperor Nero. We are able to follow the life and movements of James and Peter over the previous thirty-five years and those of Paul over the previous thirty years. The records are extensive.

It is remarkable that these men, who were to become mission leaders as a result of the change the risen Christ made in their lives, did not apparently know one another beforehand. Nor were they agreed about all things as leaders of the various Mission Teams. Differences of opinion, even quarrels between them, are a matter of record.[13] But they were united in their belief in and proclamation of the resurrection of Jesus.[14]

Critical questions are posed by the lives of these men. Why did James, Jesus' younger brother, who did not originally believe in Jesus,[15] *become* his devoted servant after

---

11 Jude 21; Hebrews 1:3; 2:9; 13:20.
12 1 Corinthians 15:3–8.
13 cf. Galatians 2:11–14; 1 Corinthians 1:12; 9:5; Acts 21:18–21.
14 1 Corinthians 15:5, 7, 8, 11.
15 John 7:5.

the First Easter? Why did Peter *continue* to serve Jesus after his death, having apparently expected the apocalyptic kingdom of God to have intervened when Jesus arrived in Jerusalem?[16] Why did Paul *begin* to serve Jesus, having been a zealous persecutor of his followers?[17]

The resurrection of Jesus from the dead is critical to these questions. Peter would not have continued, nor James and Paul have begun, to serve Jesus unless these men were convinced that Jesus had been raised from the dead.

James had remained in Nazareth with his brothers and sisters and Mary after Jesus moved to Capernaum to commence his public ministry in Galilee. It is reasonable to suppose that he, too, had been a carpenter/builder like Joseph and his older brother. There is evidence of resentment, or even of hostility, towards Jesus.[18] Yet, after the First Easter, James is found first as member, then as the first of the three pillars, then as sole leader of the Jerusalem church.[19] James had been a totally unknown Nazarene. He became leader of a community of many thousands in Jerusalem. His death is described at some length by the Jewish historian Josephus.[20]

Peter's changed lifestyle from that of an obscure fisherman in the landlocked Sea of Galilee to that of leader in an international movement whose travels took him from Galilee through Judaea, Samaria, Phoenicia, Syria, Asia Minor and Greece and Italy takes some explaining.

Consider, too, the radical turnaround of *Saul,* the obsessive protector of the faith of his fathers who, as a leading activist, sought to destroy the heretical schism associated with Jesus. But this man became the leading promoter of that very schism he had attempted to obliterate

---

16   Luke 22:38, 49; 24:21; John 18:10; Acts 1:6.
17   Galatians 1:13–16.
18   Mark 3:21, 31–35.
19   Acts 1:14; 12:17; Galatians 1:19; 2:9; Acts 15:13; 21:18.
20   *Jewish Antiquities* xx.200.

and did so among the Gentiles, a people whom, as a strict Pharisee, he would have despised for their idolatry and promiscuity. How can we account for this astonishing change? In his own words, it was because the Lord, who had been raised on the third day, appeared to him.[21]

James, Peter and Saul/Paul each served the risen Lord for about thirty years – James in Judaea, Peter and Paul on the world stage. It is very difficult to believe that they would have done this unless they were convinced that Jesus was, indeed, the risen Lord. Is it possible to be so mistaken for *thirty* years? If they were liars, would they have suffered over so long a period, and then died for their lie? Their Letters do not suggest either delusion or deceit, but clear thinking and burning integrity.

It might be argued that monks in eastern religions are prepared to die through self-immolation in the expectation of reincarnation. The leaders James, Peter and John, however, did not serve Christ and die for him in prospect of an unverifiable future life. Rather, they lived and died as they did on account of a verifiable historical event, the resurrection of Jesus. They did, indeed, die in the joyous prospect of reunion with Jesus. But it was a Jesus whom they knew had been raised from the dead because they themselves had seen him alive.

In short, the lives and the deaths of James, Peter and Paul stand as monuments to the historicity of the resurrection of Jesus.

TWO SEPARATE TRADITIONS: THE 'THIRD DAY' AND THE 'FIRST DAY'

There are two strands of information which are different in detail but not contradictory to the central fact of the

---

21   1 Corinthians 15:8–9.

resurrection. One is the tradition, quoted by Paul, that Jesus was 'raised on the third day'.[22] The other, found in each of the four Gospels, states that the women came on the 'first day of the week' to the tomb in which Jesus was buried and found it empty; the body of Jesus was not there.

Both traditions mention a *day*. The one pinpoints the resurrection day relative to the death of Jesus, the other to its occurrence in the course of the week.

Tradition 1: Jesus was 'raised on the third day'

In the mid-fifties Paul wrote reminding the Corinthians of the statement they had 'received' from him five years earlier,

> that [Christ] was raised on the third day according to the scriptures.[23]

But Paul did not compose this statement. He, too, had 'received' it as a pre-formed piece of information in the mid-thirties. Since the First Easter occurred in AD 33, this confession must have been formulated in the two to three year period between that First Easter and Paul's first visit as a Christian to Jerusalem.[24]

Jesus died and was buried mid Friday afternoon: that is, day one (part days were then counted as full days). The second day, the Sabbath, began by Jewish reckoning, at sunset on Friday and lasted until sunset on Saturday. The third day was from sunset Saturday to sunset Sunday. It was within this 'third day' that Jesus 'was raised' from the dead.

The 'third day' as a detail ties down the precise twenty-four hour period in which Jesus was raised. It was incorporated into this, the earliest creed, of Christianity,

---

22   1 Corinthians 15:3.
23   1 Corinthians 15:4; cf. Acts 10:40.
24   Galatians 1:18–19.

which Paul 'received' and which, in turn, he 'handed over' to the Corinthians.

Thus the 'third day' immediately became part of the pattern of the apostolic preaching of the Gospel of Christ. That this tradition emanated from the Jerusalem leadership to Paul is corroborated by its place in Peter's proclamation of the Gospel.[25] In the next century the 'third day' is found in the earliest forms of the 'Apostles' Creed'. Clearly the 'third day' tradition was widely proclaimed and confessed from the beginning.

Tradition 2: Jesus was raised the 'first day'

Each of the four Gospels indicates that early in the morning of the 'first day of the week' – Sunday – the women who returned to the tomb found it empty; the body of Jesus was not there.[26] Nor were the women alone in witnessing the empty tomb. Luke and John record that several of the disciples, upon hearing the report of the women, came to the tomb and found only grave cloths. Among these witnesses is John, the author of the Fourth Gospel.[27]

Jesus had died mid-afternoon Friday. The Sabbath was rapidly approaching, after which no work, such as burying a corpse, could be done. Moreover, to have left a corpse hanging at Passover Sabbath would have brought defilement to the land.[28] The problem was resolved by Joseph, a member of the Sanhedrin who was a secret follower of Jesus. He sought and received permission from the Romans to take down the body from the cross and to bury it. Joseph owned a rock tomb near to Golgotha, the site of the crucifixion.[29]

---

25 Acts 10:40.
26 Matthew 28:1–6; Mark 16:1–6; Luke 24:1–3; John 20:1–3.
27 John 20:2–8; 21:24.
28 Deuteronomy 21:23; cf. John 19:31–32.
29 Matthew 27:60.

The faithful women of Galilee, who had witnessed the death of Jesus and his interment, decided to return as soon as possible to anoint and spice the body. Early on the Sunday morning – the first day of the week – afforded the first real opportunity to do this.

But the body was gone.

The Gospel writer makes a point of saying that the disciples were 'again in the house' eight days later, that is, on the following Sunday. It seems to be established that from that time the disciples of the Lord Jesus gathered on 'the first day of the week', the 'Lord's Day'.[30] Thus from the very next Sunday after the tomb was found empty until today Christians have met together on that day as the Church of Jesus, in recognition that God raised him from the dead on that day. The Sunday gathering, therefore, is like a monument to the resurrection of the Lord.

The 'first day' tradition almost certainly rests on the recollection of the women who came to the tomb in which Jesus had been buried. The 'third day' tradition was probably influenced by Jesus' repeated prophecy that he would be raised 'after three days'. We might have expected the Gospels to narrate the discovery of the empty tomb on the 'third day', in line with so much Jesus said about the 'third day' in the Gospels.[31] But to our surprise it is the 'first day of the week' that they come to the tomb, which, because it comes so unexpectedly, enhances the credibility of the account. It is the testimony of the women that the resurrection occurred on 'the first day' which informs the four Gospels.

Jesus' words about 'three days' came to be incorporated within the church's first creed, which was formulated at Jerusalem where Paul 'received' it.[32] Peter, the disciple of Jesus who had often heard the Lord speak about the 'third

30   Acts 20:7; 1 Corinthians 16:2; Revelation 1:10.
31   John 2:19; cf. Mark 14:58; Luke 13:31–35; Matthew 12:40–41; Mark 8:31; 9:31; 10:34.
32   1 Corinthians 15:4; cf. Acts 10:40.

day' was almost certainly the source of the 'third day' tradition of Paul,[33] a tradition which he himself uses in his own gospel preaching.[34]

The two traditions, which arose separately – the one from the women, the other from the disciples – combine powerfully to reinforce the reality of the resurrection. The one, originating from the women's experience, pinpointed the day of the week when the tomb was found to be empty. The other, arising from the apostles' public proclamation,[35] which in turn was dependent on Jesus' prophecies, established which day it was relative to Jesus' death that Jesus was raised from the dead.

To this present time Christians attest the reality of the resurrection by two practices which go back to the very beginnings of the resurrection church. One is that they meet on the 'first day of the week', the 'Lord's day'. The other is that in the creed which they confess they declare that it was on the 'third day' that God raised his Son from the dead.

'ALTERNATIVE' EXPLANATIONS

A number of alternative explanations have been offered to the testimony of the New Testament, that Jesus was raised from the dead. It will be helpful to review and comment on these alternatives.

'A hoax'

There have been many spectacular hoaxes in history. Some remained unexploded for considerable periods. Not until 1953 was Charles Dawson's 1912 'Piltdown Man' finally revealed to be the remains of a very modern ape. In 1994 it

---

33 1 Corinthians 15:4; Galatians 1:18–19.
34 Acts 10:40.
35 cf. Acts 10:40.

has been finally revealed that the 1930s photo of the head of the 'monster' of Loch Ness which became known world-wide was actually a contraption made for the purpose of deception.

Was the greatest hoax of all, however, the story of the resurrection of Jesus of Nazareth? It is a story which has been believed by thousands of millions throughout the two millennia since its alleged occurrence.

Hoaxes are hard to conceal indefinitely, the more so if more than one or two perpetrators are involved, as there would have been in this case. The truth has a way of floating to the surface sooner or later.

Hoaxes, too, need the right soil and climate to take root and flourish. 'Piltdown Man' was credible enough in an era of eager interest in anthropological origins. The brooding waters of the great Scottish Loch make a 'monster' believable and it will take more than disclosures of a photographic hoax to overturn the faith of many in 'Nessie'.

But the resurrection of Jesus was, as it were, against the run of play. Jews were then expecting resurrection, but it would happen at the *end* of history and it would involve *every* person who had ever died. The scepticism of Thomas to resurrection reports was probably a typical reaction. To assert that *one* person had been raised permanently *that* day would be as unimaginable and unacceptable as announcing to the World Cup Rugby fans at half time that the game was now over and that there would be no second half.

To Greeks of the period who believed in a soul's immortality the declaration that the man Jesus had been resurrected was quite laughable.[36] The times and circumstances of 'Piltdown Man' and 'Nessie' facilitated believability, but so far as Jews and Greeks of the period were concerned, the resurrection of Jesus came straight out of left field.

---

36 Acts 17:32.

Perhaps, then, the biblical story arose from an urban myth? Did it originate somehow like the story about the man with dreadlocks who died, bitten by the redbacks which had nested in his amazing hair?

The thing about urban myths is that you can never track them down to their source. When did it happen? In which hospital? What was the man's name? The story just disappears into the fog. But it was not like that with Jesus. We know who owned the tomb where he was buried on the Friday but from which the body was missing at first light on Sunday. Nor was he a nonentity; the tomb owner was an eminent citizen of Jerusalem, Joseph from Arimathea, a member of the Supreme Council. No problem tracking him down and getting the facts. The emptiness of that tomb must be regarded as one of the most secure facts of the ancient world. That Matthew must rebut the current 'explanation' of its emptiness is evidence of that.[37]

And we also know when, where and to whom the risen Jesus presented himself. A mere twenty years after the event Paul states that more than five hundred saw him on one occasion, most of whom were alive at the time of writing.[38] In Jerusalem and Galilee he was seen alive, by Mary Magdalene and the other named women from Galilee and by the disciples whose names we know, throughout a forty-day period and by Saul some months later. The remarkable story is readily traceable at many points. This is not the stuff of urban myths.

'Another man was crucified'

The Koran, the Holy Book of Islam, holds that Jesus was a prophet. Since God would not allow his prophet to be treated that way, another man was crucified in Jesus' place. It states: 'They did not kill (Jesus) nor did they crucify him

---

37   Matthew 28:11–15.
38   1 Corinthians 15:6.

but they thought they did…it was sheer conjecture'.[39]

This explanation goes against all the evidence. It was precisely because Jesus was a public figure in Jerusalem that the Temple authorities and the Romans wanted him out of the way. Hundreds of thousands of Jewish pilgrims congregated in Jerusalem at Passover time. Past events had shown that the tiniest spark could ignite riot and tumult in so volatile a situation.

Although Jesus was arrested at night, tried before a hastily convened Sanhedrin and then brought to Pilate in the early hours of the morning, the execution was very public. Jesus, with two revolutionary activists, was crucified close to the walls of Jerusalem, near a well-used thoroughfare.[40] The very point of crucifixion was to humiliate the felon *publicly* so as to deter others from such rash behaviour.

Further, there is every indication that it was Jesus who was crucified. Those who mocked him identified him as he hung on the cross, 'He saved others…'[41] Roman soldiers were present guarding the crucified men. They would not mistake the identity of a criminal.

Soon afterwards Peter appeals to the people gathered in Jerusalem in regard to Jesus, who had been well-known to them: '*This Jesus,* whom you crucified…*this Jesus* God has raised…'[42]

It was Jesus who was crucified, not another.

'Jesus did not actually die on the cross'

The 'swoon' theory, as it is called, was argued in the early 1800s by German scholars Venturini and Paulus, and more recently by the British academic Derrett.[43] Jesus became

---

39 Koran 4:156.
40 John 19:20; Mark 15:29.
41 Mark 15:31.
42 Acts 2:36, 32.
43 J.D.M. Derrett, *The Anastasis: The Resurrection of Jesus as an Historical Event* (Shipton-on-Stour, Drinkwater, 1982).

unconscious on the cross, but revived in the tomb.

This theory is made in ignorance of the practice of crucifixion by the Romans. The Jewish historian Josephus records many instances of Roman crucifixion in Palestine. Not only was crucifixion itself violent in the extreme, it was preceded and accompanied by brutal torture. Roman soldiers took full advantage of the utter vulnerability of the victims. Sadism reigned supreme before and during crucifixion – shades of the Holocaust of the twentieth century. Taken together, the scourging and the nailing up of the victim represented an overwhelming assault on the human frame which left the person critically debilitated. Those not already dead died upon removal from the cross.

Religious art has given a false impression of the man on the cross as motionless and quietly dignified. But it would have been otherwise. Death came by asphyxiation. The downward weight of the body constricted breathing, so that the impaled constantly sought to writhe upwards to expand the lungs. The crucified used their feet and their legs to lever themselves up so as to breathe. If, however, the executioners broke the legs the victims had no leverage and thus could not breathe; death came quickly.

This is precisely what the Roman soldiers began to do late on that Friday afternoon. Bodies left impaled on the Sabbath during Passover brought defilement to the land. When the Jews requested that the three men be killed so as to permit burial before the onset of the Sabbath, the Roman soldiers began to break the legs of the victims. When they came to Jesus, however, they found that he was already dead.

One of the execution squad thrust a spear into Jesus, to gauge whether he was in fact dead, as he appeared to be. The sudden flow of blood and water was taken to be evidence of the reality of the death. Although the dead do not bleed, the blood often remains liquid in the arteries for some hours following asphyxial deaths. Depending on the

Probable crucifixion position

organs or the blood vessels pierced, for example the inferior
vena cava, water and serum could indeed issue from someone
recently deceased, especially if crucified vertically. The
Roman soldiers were trained and experienced at their grim
work.

John, author of the Fourth Gospel, was present when
Jesus breathed his last breath. He gives eyewitness testimony
that Jesus was truly dead.[44]

The body of Jesus remained on the cross until the
centurion of the execution squad had come to the prefect,
Pontius Pilate and convinced him that Jesus was dead.[45] The
prefect only released the body for burial upon the

44 John 21:24; 19:35.
45 Mark 15:43–45

131

centurion's assurances that Jesus was, indeed, dead. This was no mere formality in the case of Jesus. The brevity of the time Jesus had been crucified led the prefect to press the question whether or not he was dead. But the answers of the centurion convinced him.

All the evidence agrees that Jesus died that afternoon.

'The body was removed from the tomb'

The reason the tomb was empty, it is claimed, is that someone removed the corpse between the time of the burial late on Friday afternoon and the arrival of the women early on Sunday morning. Who might have done this and why?

Neither *Jews* nor *Romans* would have wanted the body to be other than in the tomb, as powerful evidence that the influential malefactor was indeed dead. Such was to be the fate of those who create public disturbance! Both Jews and Romans could point to the place where he was crucified and also the place where he was buried. The bones of Jesus in the tomb in which he was buried would stand as an irrefutable denial of the claims he had made and the hopes which had been invested in him.

In any case, had either Jew or Roman taken the body, they would have immediately produced it when the disciples began to proclaim that Jesus was risen.

It was widely believed at the time that the disciples had taken the body. But Matthew states that the Temple authorities bribed the Roman soldiers to say this.[46] Matthew's rebuttal of the widespread belief among the Jews that the disciples had taken the body is very clear evidence that the tomb in which Jesus had been buried did not contain his body. Indeed, throughout the next two centuries the Jewish counterclaim that the disciples had taken the body continued to be made.[47]

---

46 Matthew 28:11–15.
47 See Justin Martyr, *Dialogue with Trypho* 108 and Tertullian, *De Spectaculis* 30.

Support for this belief may be discerned in an unusual inscription erected in Nazareth at the direction of the Emperor Claudius (AD 41–54). Claudius' decree takes the draconian step whereby those who steal bodies from tombs should be subject to the death penalty. Why should Claudius have such a decree erected in Nazareth, which was a totally obscure village in the Galilee ranges? Since Claudius was a close friend of the Jewish king Herod Agrippa 1 who knew about the apostles,[48] it is reasonable to suppose that Claudius also knew about Christianity. A further indication of this is that in AD 49 Claudius expelled the Jews from Italy because they were rioting over Chrestus.[49] Claudius' Nazareth decree supports the inference in Matthew 28:11–15 that it was widely believed that the disciples had stolen the body.

That the disciples would do this is entirely improbable. The disciples had not understood Jesus' earlier words about being raised after three days.[50] As Jews they believed in the *universal* resurrection of everyone who had ever died which will occur at the *end* of history. Martha told Jesus that her brother would rise again in *the* resurrection in *the last day*.[51] This was Jewish orthodoxy, to which the disciples would have subscribed. An individual's permanent resurrection now, *before* the end of history, would have been unimaginable, quite outside their well-established frame of reference.

It would, indeed, be like a Football Final where, without warning and against all expectations, the officials announced at half time that the game had now finished and there would be no second half.

The disciples had come armed to Jerusalem[52] expecting a

---

48 Acts 12: 1–5.
49 So Suetonius, *Claudius* 25.4; cf. Acts 18:2; Suetonius' *Chrestus* is held to be misspelling of *Christus*.
50 Mark 9:10.
51 John 11:24.
52 Luke 22:49–50; John 19:10; cf. Luke 19:11.

messianic showdown.[53] They did not expect Jesus to be raised because they did not expect him to be killed. By definition the Messiah was a victor and they had come with him to share in the spoils of his apocalyptic triumph. On the way to Jerusalem, James and John wanted to have places of power when he entered into his glory.[54] Jesus' words about his death and resurrection as they travelled to Jerusalem fell on deaf ears.[55] The report of the women, that the tomb was empty and that Jesus' promise that he would be raised the third day had been fulfilled, was greeted by the disciples with disbelief as an idle tale.[56]

The suggestion, then, that these deeply disappointed men, steeped in an apocalyptic world-view, suddenly thought of stealing the body and saying that Jesus, as an *individual,* had been raised from the dead before the onset of the end of the world is extremely improbable.

In any case, this proposition raises as many questions as it answers. Why did not one of the eleven break ranks and expose the fraud? Why would these men be prepared to die as martyrs for something they knew to be untrue? How can we explain the transparent call for goodness and truth which permeates the entire New Testament, if the whole enterprise was a conspiracy?

'The women returned to the wrong tomb'

This alternative explanation states that the women made the simplest of mistakes. They returned to the wrong tomb, found it empty and declared that the Lord had risen.[57]

By the time Jesus had died it was mid to late afternoon; a new day, the Sabbath, would soon begin. With the rapid

---

53 Acts 1:6; cf. Luke 24:21.
54 Mark 10:35–37.
55 Mark 9:10; 10:32.
56 Luke 24:11.
57 A view associated with Kirsopp Lake, *The Historical Evidence for the Resurrection of Jesus,* (New York, Putnam, 1907).

onset of the Passover Sabbath Jesus must be taken from the cross and interred, otherwise the land would be defiled.[58] The records show that Joseph of Arimathea, a member of the Sanhedrin, made his as yet unused tomb available for the burial of Jesus.[59] It is clear from the records that Joseph's tomb was close to Golgotha, the site of the crucifixion.[60] Golgotha itself was close to the walls of Jerusalem; the *titulus,* or caption attached to Jesus' cross, could be read from the city wall.[61] In other words, the tomb was readily locatable, being (1) close to Jesus' cross which was in turn close to the city walls, and (2) doubtless a substantial tomb, belonging to one of the most prominent members of the community. Each Gospel tells us that the tomb to which the women came and which they found to be empty belonged to a man of high profile with whom the story could be readily checked.

Moreover, the Gospels indicate that the women sat opposite the tomb so that they saw 'where' and 'how' the burial occurred.[62] The 'mistaken tomb' hypothesis is improbable and goes against the considerable evidence given for the burial of Jesus.

But disciples also came to the tomb, on the report of the women.[63] John, author of the Fourth Gospel, was one of those who came to the tomb. He testifies as an eyewitness that only Jesus' burial cloths were in the tomb.[64] The presence of burial cloths confirms that the women had, indeed, come to the right place. Clearly they had come to the tomb in which Jesus had been buried.

---

58 Deuteronomy 21:23; John 19:31, 42.
59 Matthew 27:60.
60 John 19:40, 42.
61 John 19:20.
62 Matthew 27:61; Mark 15:47; Luke 23:55.
63 Luke 24:24.
64 John 20:5–8.

'The resurrection stories are legendary'

It is well established that legends take many years – in fact decades and centuries – to develop.

But the 'first day of the week' tradition arises from the women who went to the tomb. It became fixed immediately, as the significant day of the week, because from the beginning the disciples began to meet on that day, the 'first day of the week', to commemorate the Lord's resurrection.[65]

The 'third day' tradition is also able to be fixed in time. It was well established by the mid-thirties when Paul 'received' it from the hands of the leaders of the Jerusalem Church.

This is not the stuff of legends, but of history. These markers – the 'first day of the week' and the 'on the third day' – arose immediately after, and for no other reason than, the event of the resurrection of Jesus.

'The resurrection originated in the Osiris myth'

Some people argue that the Egyptian Myth of Isis and Osiris is the real source of the New Testament proclamation of the resurrection of Jesus. The ancient Egyptian myth of Isis and Osiris, in a Hellenised form, became a widely followed cult around the Mediterranean world in the centuries after Alexander's conquest of Egypt in the fourth century before Christ.

According to the myth Osiris, who had been a pharaoh, was murdered and mutilated by his brother Set. Isis, Osiris' sister and wife, collected and buried his remains and caused him to be reanimated as the god of the dead. Thus Osiris reigns over the underworld as a mummy; his 'new life' is a replica of earthly life.

The association of Jesus with Osiris was fashionable in earlier generations, largely through the influence of James

---

65 John 20:26; cf. Acts 20:7; 1 Corinthians 16:2.

Frazer's *The Golden Bough,* published in 1906. The German scholar Rudolph Bultmann advocated a version of the dying and rising god as the explanation of the resurrection of Jesus. Bultmann's supposed parallels, however, all postdate the New Testament by several hundred years.

Few today pursue this line of thought.

We should note that (1) the grotesque story of Isis and Osiris is quite unlike the account of the resurrection of Jesus; (2) as devout Jews, and therefore monotheists, the disciples would have had no part in an idolatrous Gentile cult or its beliefs; (3) the account of Jesus gives people, time and place specifics which, by their nature, are not found in myths, which are ahistorical; (4) the formal credo about the resurrection of Jesus had been established within so brief a period as two or three years from the event; and (5) Jesus is not a reanimated god over the nether regions; rather, he is alive for evermore, the Lord both of the dead and the living.[66]

JESUS APPEARED ALIVE FROM THE DEAD ON MANY OCCASIONS

According to the Acts of the Apostles, Jesus, after his sufferings

> gave many convincing proofs that he was alive. He appeared to them over a period of forty days.[67]

Within the New Testament there are five narratives of the appearances of the risen Jesus – Paul's and the four Gospel writers'.

---

66   Revelation 1:18; Romans 14:9.
67   Acts 1:3.

Paul (1 Corinthians 15:3–8):

This letter can be dated at AD 55 and probably pre-dates the writing of the Gospels.

Paul's words, however, are not his own. He is quoting a pre-formed set of statements about Christ which he 'received', almost certainly in the mid-thirties from the hands of the leaders of the Jerusalem Church.[68] These statements, therefore, are very close to Jesus, and were formulated within two years of the First Easter:

> *what* I received I passed on to you...
> *that* Christ died for our sins according to the scriptures,
> *that* he was buried,
> *that* he was raised on the third day according to the scriptures
> and *that* he appeared to Cephas,
> then to the Twelve.
> Then he appeared to more than five hundred...at the one time, most of whom are still living, though some have fallen asleep.
> Then he appeared to James,
> then to all the apostles
> and last of all he appeared also to me...

Paul's *'what'* signifies something objective, an entity, a raft of four facts.[69] This *'what'* is then expanded upon by four statements each introduced by *'that'*. Each *that* (Greek: *hoti*) signifies a separate statement in quotation marks (Greek language then lacked punctuation marks).

But the four statements are logically interconnected: Christ died *and* was buried *and* was raised on the third day *and* appeared to various people. The four statements are of a piece; they form one complete statement about what

---

68   Galatians 1:18–19; cf. 2:8–9.
69   cf. 1 Corinthians 11:23 – 'For I received from the Lord *what* I also delivered to you...'

happened to Christ at the time of the First Easter. He died, was buried, was raised, appeared.

Each statement depends on its predecessor: Christ appeared *because* he had been raised; he was raised *because* he had been buried; he was buried *because* he had died.

Having died, Christ was *entombed* (Greek: *etaphē*).[70] The words which follow imply that the tomb was empty.

He was *raised* on the *third* day. Paul's Greek here betrays an underlying Aramaic form of words, literally 'Christ...was raised in the day the third'. The uncorrected Greek echoes the confession of the Aramaic-speaking community in Jerusalem from whom Paul received it.

He *appeared* on six occasions, the *then...then...then...then... last of all*, suggesting due sequence. The first two probably occurred in *Jerusalem,* the third and fourth in *Galilee,* the fifth in Jerusalem and the sixth – to Saul – near *Damascus.*

The names of those to whom he *appeared* – and *was seen by* – are either given (*Cephas* = Peter, *the Twelve, James, Paul*) or are able to be readily ascertained (the five hundred, all the apostles). The witnesses to this event can be interrogated, including the vast number of five hundred who saw the risen Christ on one occasion. This is no urban myth. The sources of this remarkable event are identified and accessible. Let those who doubt go and enquire of these people themselves.

There is nothing vague here. The language is specific. Paul's is a statement of remarkable precision. It gives the lie to various 'explanations' – which are really rationalisations – like the 'swoon' theory, or the 'wrong tomb' theory, the 'mistaken identity' theory or the 'stolen body' theory.

---

70 cf. Acts 13:29. The Gospel of Matthew refers to the burial chamber as *taphos* (27:61, 64, 66; 28:1).

John (John 19:33–35; 20:4–8, 19–23):

John, the author of the Fourth Gospel also claims, like Paul, to have seen the risen Christ. He testifies to having seen Jesus die, to have come to the empty tomb where he saw the burial cloths and to have seen the risen Lord.

Of the four Gospel writers, this writer devotes the greatest space to the resurrection appearances of Jesus (chapters 20–21 – 56 verses). The risen Jesus appeared to Mary Magdalene on the first day of the week (Sunday). Later that day he appeared to the disciples, Thomas being absent. Eight days later, the next Sunday by inclusive counting, he appeared again to the disciples, Thomas now being present. On one other occasion, noted as the third to his disciples, Jesus appeared in Galilee, by the Sea of Tiberias, to seven of his disciples, five of whom are named.

However, John is not writing primarily to convince his readers about the truth of the resurrection, but more particularly to establish the character of Jesus' resurrection body. As raised from the dead, Jesus had a physical body, but it was not limited in its movements. Nor was Jesus destined to remain here. He must go to his Father in order that another 'comforter', the Holy Spirit, may come. True as it is that Thomas' doubt is exposed to show that there can be no doubt, John also writes to underline the importance of faith based on the word rather than by sight. Furthermore, John also wishes to highlight Peter's special future role in feeding Christ's sheep. Clearly, John writes to establish these things rather than narrate or prove the resurrection of Jesus.

Luke (Luke 24:1–52):

Luke gives the next greatest volume of information about Jesus' resurrection appearances (chapter 24 – 52 verses).

Luke (1) notes that Jesus had appeared to Peter, (2) narrates at length his conversation with Cleopas and another man walking to Emmaus, (3) recounts Jesus' meeting with the Eleven in Jerusalem, and (4) his final contact with them at Bethany.

As with John, Luke is not attempting to establish the fact of the resurrection. That he assumes. Rather, Luke is narrating the appearances of Jesus so as to teach about the nature of Jesus' resurrected person. On one hand Jesus is risen as a physical body (he eats, drinks, shows his wounds); but, on the other, he is not now limited by physical constraints. Luke is preparing his readers for the eventual absence of Jesus, when he will not be present with them. This he records in his second volume, the Acts of the Apostles.

Nonetheless, though it may not have been his primary intention, Luke's account, like John's, does serve powerfully to establish the fact of the resurrection.

Matthew (Matthew 28:1-20):

Matthew records two appearances of the risen Jesus – one to the faithful Galilean women in Jerusalem, the other to the Eleven in Galilee.

Matthew assumes, rather than seeks to prove, the fact of the resurrection. His point, instead, is to show that Jesus is now to be worshipped as the One who has all authority and that the message about him is to be taken to the nations. It will be remembered that he is introduced as the Christ in the opening chapters, who as a child is then worshipped by representatives from the nations, the *magi*. The resurrection appearances, in both of which Jesus is worshipped, form a fitting conclusion and climax to the entire Gospel of Matthew.

Mark (Mark 16:1-8):

Mark gives no account of a resurrection appearance. Nonetheless, it is clear that Jesus will be seen by the disciples in Galilee. The tomb is empty. Jesus is not where he was buried; he is risen.

Mark is not intent on proving the fact of the resurrection. As with the other Gospel writers, this is something he assumes. Rather, Mark is seeking to rivet our attention on the future and final appearance of Jesus. His dramatic account of the emptiness of the tomb, the absence of Jesus and the awestruck fear of the women which dominate the final sentences of the Gospel take the reader to the edge of the eschatological abyss. We will not see Jesus again until his *parousia*. To have recounted resurrection appearances would have been a distraction so far as Mark's purposes are concerned.

Summary: resurrection appearances

There are five narratives of Jesus' resurrection appearances. Yet none of them sets out, as its primary intention, to prove the fact of the resurrection. Paul merely repeats what the Corinthians already believe to demonstrate the inconsistency of doubting the resurrection of *their* bodies. The Gospel writers each has his own point to make as he narrates these appearances, or, even, in Mark's case, Jesus' *non*-appearance.

In each narrative, names are given of those to whom the risen Christ presented himself. Astonishing as the story of Jesus' resurrection is, it is no urban myth, which by its nature disappears into the fog leaving the story unverifiable. Let the reader understand that the sources can be traced and checked.

From these five accounts we can list twelve known separate occasions when the risen Christ appeared to individuals or groups. This is the more impressive when it is noted that these narratives arise from separate and independent traditions.

1 Corinthians 15	John 20	Luke 24	Matthew 28	Number of appearances
	(v.15) Mary			1
			(v.6) women	2
[Christ] appeared to (v.5) Cephas		(v.34) Simon		3
		(v.15) 2 men		4
next (v.5) to the Twelve	(v.17) disciples [1]	(v.36) disciples		5
	(v.26) disciples [2]			6
	John 21 (v.1) 7 disciples [3]			7
next (v.6) to 500+			(v.16) disciples in Galilee	8
				9
next (v.7) to James		(v.50) disciples		10
next to all the Apostles				11
last of all (v.8) to Paul				12

Resurrection appearances of the risen Christ

143

While there is some uncertainty as to the precise sequence, we may say that the risen Christ appeared on at least twelve separate occasions, to both individuals and to groups. He was seen, heard and touched at different times and places. The names of those to whom he appeared are either given or at least readily ascertainable.

It has to be admitted that there is some difficulty harmonising the accounts of the resurrection appearances as recorded in our sources,[71] something which has been cited as evidence of unreliability. It should be pointed out, however, that neither Paul nor the Gospel writers are setting out to prove or even to systematically narrate the history of Jesus' resurrection appearances. These authors write from the assumption that their readers know about and believe the resurrection. Furthermore, the very existence of 'loose ends' is evidence that these writers have not contrived a harmonious, even account. The discrepancies are a reason to believe in the naive integrity of the writers and, indeed, are not unusual in writers of the period. Three historians who narrate the Great Fire of Rome in AD 64 disagree about Nero's whereabouts during the fire and whether he 'fiddled' (i.e. played the lyre) or sang while the city burned. But no one seriously doubts that Nero failed to show leadership during the disaster or that he either sang or played while the city was being destroyed.

In short, the fact of the resurrection appearances of Jesus to so many people and at different times and places as recorded by Paul and the Gospel writers argues powerfully for the truth of the resurrection. Remarkably, the information is given gratuitously, almost casually, as if its incontrovertible nature is axiomatic. In each case the writer is wanting to go beyond the fact of the resurrection to make another point.

---

71 But see J. Wenham, *Easter Enigma. Do the Resurrection Stories Contradict One Another?* (Exeter, Paternoster, 1984).

144

'ALTERNATIVES' TO THE PHYSICAL
RESURRECTION OF JESUS

It is quite clear that something left its mark in history in early April AD 33.

Some who find the notion of Jesus' bodily resurrection unacceptable opt for some other alternative, either (1) that the disciples saw Jesus in some kind of visionary sense[72] or (2) that Jesus' body was *spiritual,* not physical or (3) that the disciples underwent a 'resurrection' as they reflected further on Jesus' death in the weeks after the event.

In regard to the first explanation, it must be realised that Jesus appeared to both individuals and groups in various places over a forty day period. They ate with him and touched him. They heard as well as saw him. The risen Jesus did not exist in their minds, but was encountered objectively and physically, external to them.

From the psychological viewpoint this explanation of a resurrection in some visionary sense runs contrary to the situation as it was that Passover. The disciples had expected a messianic coup, a divine intervention to bring in the Kingdom of God.[73] The arrest and execution of their leader left them demoralised and afraid at first to go out of doors.[74] They greeted the news of Jesus' resurrection as stupid.[75] They were not, in fact, psychologically conditioned for this supposed vision or hallucination.

The New Testament knows the difference between seeing the risen Lord and a vision of the Lord. There are a number of visions of the Lord referred to in the New Testament, for example, by Stephen and by Paul.[76] But what these people saw during these forty days, and Paul after that, was no

---

72 Associated with the views of E. Renan, *The Life of Jesus* (ET New York, Doubleday, 1904).
73 Luke 24:19–21.
74 John 20:19.
75 Luke 24:11.
76 Acts 7:56; 18:9.

vision, but the objectively risen person, Jesus.

Some scholars advocate a second (spiritual) explanation on the basis of Paul's words in 1 Corinthians that because the body is raised as a *spiritual* body, and that flesh and blood cannot inherit the kingdom of God,[77] Christ must have been raised as a *spiritual,* non-physical body.

But in the passage in question,[78] Paul is not discussing Christ's resurrected body, but the believers' resurrection body. Christ was not 'natural' or 'unspiritual' in his understanding; quite the reverse. Nor was he 'flesh and blood', that is, lacking the strength of God to do God's will or to resist evil;[79] again, the reverse is true. Uniquely filled with the Spirit of God, Jesus was the very embodiment on earth of the kingdom of God. Humans need to be transformed to be fit for the kingdom of God; Jesus Christ did not.

In any case, Paul's contrast is not between a physical and a spiritual body, but literally between the human this-worldly or 'natural' *(psychikos)* body and the supernatural or *spiritual (pneumatikos)* body. The former body is for this age, 'natural', 'unregenerate';[80] the latter, which is now Spirit-dominated, is for the coming age.

The view (3) that the disciples had a kind of spiritual resurrection in the aftermath of the crucifixion, as they came to see Jesus 'alive', has been advanced recently by Bishop Spong.[81] Spong holds that there was no empty tomb because Jesus was thrown into a common grave, and there were no appearances because the corpse remained dead. Rather, Spong states that Peter, once back in Galilee, on reflecting on the crucifixion, himself underwent a 'resurrection', believing that Jesus was now 'alive'. It was Peter, not Jesus, who was

77 1 Corinthians 15:44, 50.
78 1 Corinthians 15:35ff.
79 Ephesians 6:12; Matthew 16:17.
80 See 1 Corinthians 2:14 RSV.
81 J.S. Spong, *Resurrection: Myth or Reality* (San Franscisco, Harper Collins, 1994).

'resurrected'. One wonders how Spong's view is different from those who believe, somehow, that Elvis 'still lives'? Or John Kennedy, or Charles de Gaulle?

Spong holds that Jesus was exalted direct from the grave to the right hand of God. Thus Paul and the other witnesses cited by him[82] did not see the Jesus who was resurrected from the grave, but a heavenly vision, a revelation. Spong repudiates as 'literalising' any interpretations of resurrection in physical terms. Resurrection, he claims, is about a heavenly revelation, not a resuscitated corpse.

But the apostles preached 'the resurrection *of the dead*', not a spiritual exaltation of Jesus 'from the grave to the right hand of God', as Spong has suggested.

Spong's view that Jesus' body remained in the grave is entirely at odds with the testimony of the apostles Peter and Paul, whose missionary speeches are quoted in the Acts of the Apostles in chapters two and thirteen.[83] Both apostles insist that Jesus was buried in a tomb but that, in fulfilment of Psalm 16, the flesh of God's Holy One did not see corruption. Rather, God raised him *physically* from the dead.

David, the author of that Psalm is, indeed, dead. The location of David's tomb, which contained his mortal remains, was still known (and venerated?) at that time. But Jesus, the Holy One whose coming David had prophesied, did not see corruption. David saw corruption following his death, but Jesus whom he prophesied, did not. On the contrary, Jesus appeared alive from the dead to those who had accompanied him from Galilee, who now bear witness to his resurrection from the dead. Both apostles, quoting as they do Psalm 16, make it crystal clear that Jesus was raised physically from the dead.

Whom are we to believe? The apostles Peter and Paul, who were contemporaries of the original Easter Event, or our contemporary, the Bishop of Newark?

---

82   1 Corinthians 15:3–8.
83   See Acts 2:23–32; 13:29–37.

A RADICAL NEW ZEAL FOR THE LORD

Zeal for the Lord, a life and death commitment to the covenant God of Israel, characterised the Jewish people in the era of Jesus.

For centuries they had been surrounded by the ghastly religious and ethical culture of the Gentiles, whether in the Graeco-Roman cities of the eastern Mediterranean or even within the Holy Land. Jerusalem itself was subject to the corrupting presence of the Gentiles. Wherever they looked, Jews were confronted with Gentile religion and practices which were abhorrent to them.

To preserve the honour of Yahweh and their own distinctive identity as His people they would die rather than break the Sabbath, violate their food laws, leave their sons uncircumcised, sit at table with a Gentile or allow their Temple to be desecrated. During Jesus' century, hundreds of thousands of his countrymen would die defending the Holy Name of Yahweh, their God. Such was their zeal for the One who was jealous for the undivided loyalty of His people.

Saul of Tarsus – the pre-Christian Paul – provides a good example of this zeal for Yahweh, which would, if necessary, yield its own life for Yahweh and take the lives of others. This extreme Jewish fundamentalism was the norm among Jews of the period.

It is a secure fact of history that, following the First Easter, there was a group of Jews who retained their zeal for Yahweh, but who now expressed it as *zeal for Jesus*. Jesus called for his followers to take up a cross, that is, to be prepared to die for *him*. The records show that many Jews, named and unnamed, did in fact die out of this re-defined, re-directed zeal, which was zeal for Jesus.

At the same time their zeal for Judaism was significantly qualified, even though they remained Jews. They continued to observe the Sabbath, *and* to meet on the first day of the week. They retained their involvement in synagogue and Temple *and* they met in households and as churches. They observed the Levitical food laws, *but* were not bound by them. They continued to circumcise their sons, *but* allowed Gentile believers the liberty not to do so. They customarily ate with with fellow-Jews, *but* were able to eat also with Gentiles. They remained domiciled in Jerusalem, *but* they did not remain there armed, to defend the Holy City, but withdrew to a place of safety until the end of the war.

The changed attitudes of these Jews who were Christians are matters of record. This change is remarkable since it was by their tenacious conservatism in matters related to the Temple and the Torah (= Law of Moses) that Jews preserved themselves as the covenantal people of Yahweh. Yet something had happened to make these Jewish Christians change in these fundamentals.

That 'something' was *someone,* Jesus of Nazareth. But not merely his own remarkable person, but the resurrection of that person from the dead. As one eminent scholar put it:

> one is bound to recognise something startlingly novel, and to ask what there is to account for it. And the answer seems to be a most powerful and original mind, and a tremendous confirmatory event.[84]

Other leaders had arisen within that century, with followers more numerous by far than those who attended Jesus. Yet when these leaders died, their movements stopped immediately and their followers dispersed. But those who followed Jesus before the First Easter continued to follow him after Easter, with no interruption and with rapidly increased numbers. How can we account for this, apart from Jesus' resurrection from the dead and the coming of the Holy Spirit?

Jesus' followers now expressed their zeal for Yahweh as zeal for Jesus, as a life and death loyalty to him. But the

---

84 C.F.D. Moule, *The Phenomenon of the New Testament* (London, SCM, 1967), 17.

elements of Judaism, which had been the means by which they had primarily expressed their zeal for Yahweh, were now secondary.

The unique person of Jesus was validated to his original disciples by his resurrection from the dead. It is this – as a fact of history – which gives the most intellectually satisfying explanation for the radically redirected zeal of the Jews who were also Christians in the generation after Jesus. Indeed, apart from the resurrection of Jesus, the survival, indeed the growth, of early Christianity, is inexplicable. As Professor C.F.D. Moule wrote:

> If the coming into existence of the Nazarenes, a phenomenon undeniably attested by the New Testament, rips a great hole in history, a hole the size and shape of the Resurrection, what does the secular historian propose to stop it up with?[85]

THE CHALLENGE OF THE EVIDENCE

The analysis of the resurrection belongs to disciplines which evaluate evidence, in particular those of the historian and the lawyer. An eminent historian of the period, Paul L. Maier, with due care, gave this opinion:

> If all the evidence is weighed carefully and fairly, it is indeed justifiable, according to the canons of historical research, to conclude that the tomb in which Jesus was buried was actually empty on the morning of the First Easter. And no shred of evidence has yet been discovered in literary sources, epigraphy or archaeology that would disprove this statement.[86]

The discipline of legal prosecution closely resembles that

---

85 *Phenomenon*, 3.
86 Cited in private correspondence to Josh McDowell.

of the historian. Both must weigh and evaluate evidence as a basis for arriving at a reasonable conclusion. A noted jurist, Sir Edward Clarke, commented that:

> The evidence for [the events of the first Easter Day] is conclusive, and over and over again in the High Court I have secured the verdict on evidence not nearly so compelling…a truthful witness is always artless and disdains effect. The Gospel evidence for the resurrection is of this class and, as a lawyer, I accept it unreservedly as the testimony of truthful men to facts they were able to substantiate.[87]

Let each one of us honestly face the evidence for the resurrection and reach our own conclusions. Reduced to basics, the alternatives are either (1) that one has to accept the evidence as true or (2) to conclude that an elaborate fraud has been perpetrated on the human race. But for me, the quality of the evidence and the moral tone of the literature in which it occurs, lead me to conclude that Jesus, having been killed was, after three days, raised from the dead on the first day of Passover week.

Sunday, 5 April AD 33.

The first day in God's new world order.

---

87   Quoted in J. Stott, *Basic Christianity* (Leicester, IVP, 1974), 47.

QUESTIONS FOR REFLECTION AND DISCUSSION:

1. How important is the factuality of the resurrection of Jesus for Christianity?

2. Would belief in Jesus' resurrection have been culturally acceptable at that time (i) to Jews, (ii) to Gentiles?

3. What is for you the most powerful evidence for Jesus' resurrection?

FURTHER READING:

W.L. Craig, *Apologetics* (Chicago, Moody Press, 1984).

W.L. Craig, 'The Empty Tomb of Jesus', in R.T. France and D. Wenham, *Gospel Perspectives* Vol. 2 (Sheffield, JSOT,1981).

M. Harris, *Raised Immortal* (Grand Rapids, Eerdmans, 1985).

M. Harris, *Three Crucial Questions* (Grand Rapids, Eerdmans, 1994).

G.E. Ladd, *I Believe in the Resurrection of Jesus* (London, Hodder & Stoughton, 1975).

Chapter Nine

Who, then, is Jesus?

Every reader of the Gospels should ask and seek to answer this question.

As we turn the pages of the Gospels we see people struggling with the enigmatic figure who stands before them. The disciples asked themselves, 'Who, then, is this?' Herod Antipas, the fox-like ruler of Galilee-Peraea, thought that, somehow, Jesus was John the Baptist come back from the dead. Jesus' own family said he was 'beside himself', deranged. The religious establishment concluded that he was Satanic.

It is a measure of the Gospels' genuineness that they allow us to hear Jesus' contemporaries reaching a range of conclusions about Jesus, including such negative ones. Nonetheless, each Gospel writer positions the readers before Jesus so that they, too – like Peter, the centurion and Thomas – will confess Jesus to be the Son of God.[1]

Who, then, is this Jesus?

The Gospel writers play a critical role in regard to readers reaching their decision concerning the truth about Jesus. It is through the Gospels that we meet Jesus as the Son of God and are encouraged to confess him as the Son of God.

Logically speaking, there appear to be four possibilities in regard to the Gospels' evidence about Jesus: (1) Jesus did not claim to be the Son of God; (2) Jesus was self-deluded in his belief that he was the Son of God; (3) Jesus made bogus

---

1   Matthew 16:16; Mark 15:39; John 20:28.

claims to be the Son of God, knowing that he wasn't; (4) Jesus was, indeed, the Son of God.

Option 1: 'Jesus made no claims to be the Son of God'

According to this option Jesus did not claim to be the Son of God, but the Gospels have, nonetheless, so portrayed him.

Fashions change as to the perceptions of Jesus. Many today take as their point of departure Jesus' *Jewishness*. Those who take this view tend to see Jesus in one or other of two roles.

For some, Jesus was a Galilean holy man who taught the way of truth, but who was cruelly martyred by the religious leaders of his day. This Jesus, as a devout mystic, has been the preferred option of liberal Christians and Jews for many years, going back to the previous century. He fulfils the humanistic ideal for the religious and good man. He presents no demands, poses no threat to personal autonomy. Jesus as devout mystic is associated with the writings of Geza Vermes, as popularized by the biographer–novelist A.N. Wilson.[2]

For others, however, Jesus the 'pale Galilean', beloved of nineteenth century idealists, is so innocuous as to have left no mark at all in history. He could not have been the genuinely historical Jesus, had he been so anaemic. Thus, at the other extreme, to have made the impact he did Jesus must have been a fiery apocalyptist who predicted the imminent end of the world heralded by the coming of the heavenly Son of Man. This version of Jesus was classically expressed at the beginning of the twentieth century by Albert Schweitzer, and more recently and with modifications by E.P. Sanders.[3]

---

2   G. Vermes, *Jesus the Jew* (London, Collins, 1973); A.N. Wilson, *Jesus* (London, Sinclair–Davidson, 1992).

3   A. Schweitzer, *The Quest of the Historical Jesus* (English trans: London, A.& C. Black, 1954); E.P. Sanders, *Jesus and Judaism* (London, SCM, 1985).

Neither of these interpretations countenances the view that Jesus was the unique Son of God. This Jesus is the creation of the Gospel writers in the years that followed.

But we must ask, why would the Gospel writers want to make a devout rabbi or an apocalyptist into the Son of God, if he was not? There were such rabbis and apocalyptists contemporary with Jesus. No such claims were made for them. Why would they be made for Jesus?

Not all see Jesus' Jewishness as the critical element. Some, for example, see him as influenced by and propagating one of the Greek schools of those times, namely, the pungent philosophy of the cynics.[4] Again, we must ask, if Jesus was merely a Cynic philosopher, how was early Christianity launched? And why is there little if any trace of Cynic thought in the mission Letters? And is it feasible to suggest, as those who promote this view suggest, that the Gospels are from start to finish works of imagination?

Let us be reminded that we are not dependent on one record; we have four. As we have said in Chapter 4, these writings are not remote in time from Jesus, not cut off from him. Matthew and John were disciples. Mark and Luke were at one remove from Jesus, the former dependent on oral testimony, the latter dependent on written. Both Mark and Luke received their information about Jesus from disciples of Jesus. The Gospels were written out of living connection with Jesus, they are the living link between Jesus and succeeding generations.

Moreover, the Gospel of John is so unlike the style and emphasis of the other three that we must take it to have been written independently of the others.

To discredit the Gospels as a means to denying Jesus' identity as the Son of God is, in our opinion, a desperate strategy. If these writers have deceptively portrayed Jesus

---

4   See e.g. B.H. Mack, *A Myth of Innocence: Mark and Christian Origins* (Philadelpia, Fortress, 1988).

they forfeit any claim to be taken seriously at any point. If deception lies at their heart as historical documents they are of little, if any, value. It is quite inconsistent for scholars to argue that the Gospel writers have deceived us and then proceed to use those same writings as a basis for their own versions of Jesus as devout rabbi or fiery apocalyptist or Cynic philosopher, or whatever else they may think of.

Option 2: 'Jesus was deluded in his claim to be the son of God'

Essentially, this option questions Jesus' sanity. To claim, in all sincerity, to be the Son of God when one is not, implies psychological imbalance.

But that is what we must say of someone who believed that he had the right to forgive *other* people their sins, that to follow him would bring eternal life, that he would be the judge of all mankind on the last day and that he was, uniquely, the Son of God if he in all truth was not the Son of God.

Society has often taken the view that those who hold such views are a danger to themselves and need to be isolated from others. Jim Jones and David Koresh believed they were messiahs. If Jesus was deluded, his delusion was the more intense. Jesus believed that he was God with us. To be true to the record, Jesus' own family questioned his sanity and the religious leaders accused him of 'mania', of 'raving'.[5] But the goodness and power of Jesus' life and miracles reflected the folly of these charges.

The difficulty with this hypothesis, whether expressed then or now, is that at every other point where he speaks and acts, Jesus displays penetrating insight. This option expects us to believe that, while the inner logic and consistency of Jesus' teaching in every other area is

---

5   Mark 3:21; John 10:20.

overpowering, in regard to himself, Jesus is self-deluded. This is the fatal flaw with option 2.

Whatever else he was, Jesus was not insane.

Option 3: 'Jesus made bogus claims'

These options represent diminishing views of Jesus. In Option 1, because he makes no claims to be the Son of God, we take a morally neutral view of Jesus. In Option 2, because he is deluded, we may feel a measure of pity towards him. In Option 3, however, because he deliberately deceives us, we feel only contempt.

To masquerade as the Son of God incarnate would, indeed, be a Satanic deception.

Again, to be true to the records, the religious establishment did indeed accuse him of being a blasphemer, a sinner, a false teacher who led the people astray and, indeed, as one who was demon-empowered.[6]

But this option, too, had then, and has now, nothing to support it. As Jesus himself said, 'How can Satan cast out Satan?'[7] His entire ministry confronted and overcame evil in all its forms – ignorance, malevolence and suffering. Blinding purity and integrity and his own utter contempt for hypocrisy is what impress us about Jesus. To attribute religious fraud of the most profound kind to Jesus is incomprehensible.

If he is evil, why is he pitted against evil?

Option 4: 'Jesus is the Son of God'

A passage which neatly raises the issues of Jesus' identity is Mark's account of the interchange between Jesus and his disciples at Caesarea Philippi.[8] When Jesus asked the

---

6 John 7:12; 9:16; 10:21; Mark 2:7.
7 Mark 3:23.
8 Mark 8:27–9:1.

disciples who the people thought he was they reported that the general populace concluded that he was John the Baptist or one of the Old Testament prophets who had, somehow, come back into history. In the public perception Jesus was a prophet.

But, when he asked them who they thought he was, they – through Peter – replied that he was 'the Christ', the long awaited 'Messiah' of the Lord.

This, too, was a widely held view. The religious authorities asked him whether or not he said he was the Christ.[9] Upon his arrest, those who accused him before the Roman prefect made precisely this charge, though in political terms which the Romans would understand.[10] He was found guilty and executed as 'King of the Jews'.[11] The secular historians Josephus and Tacitus corroborate that it was as the Christ that Jesus was executed by the Roman authorities.

But, according to the passage in Mark chapter 8, Jesus rejects the disciples' identification of him as the Christ/the Messiah. There is ample evidence that Jews of the period expected the Messiah to be a military victor who would give the covenant people of Yahweh deliverance from the Gentiles. Jesus will not accept this military and triumphalist role from the disciples, though on the eve of his crucifixion he did not deny that he was the Messiah.

To the disciples, who were looking for God's apocalyptic intervention in history, Jesus spoke of himself as the Son of Man, who called God, 'my Father'. According to Jesus, he is the Son of Man – God's Special Man – who is the Son of God, God's own Son. As the Gospel of Mark progresses, Jesus will refer to himself as 'beloved Son', and as 'the Son' and to God as 'Abba, Father'.[12] He will be rejected in

9 John 10:24.
10 Mark 14:62; 15:2.
11 Luke 23:2–5; Mark 15:26.
12 Mark 12:6; 13:32.

158

Jerusalem by the Temple hierarchy, executed by the Gentiles, but after three days rise from the dead. And he will, at some point after the destruction of the Temple, return in glory with the holy angels.

Thus from Mark 8:27–9:1 we see, in turn, who the crowd and the disciples thought Jesus was. Finally, we hear from his own lips his own assertion of his identity, the Son of Man – God's Special Man for this, God's special time – who is the Son of God.

It is as the Son of God that Mark introduces him in his opening words and it is as the Son of God that God acknowledges him and the demons recognise him. And, finally, it is as the Son of God that the Roman centurion confesses him.[13]

Clearly Mark is convinced that Jesus is the Son of God and he wants his readers to share his conviction.

But from whom did this writer learn that Jesus was the Son of God? Not from the multitudes, nor, equally from the original attitudes of the disciples. It was Jesus himself who revealed himself as the Son of God and the disciples – with the help of God – came to believe it.[14] Jesus is the source of his true identity; the disciples, and through them those who wrote the Gospels, have it from Jesus.

And the resurrection of Jesus from the dead validated his self-revelation.

Who, then, is this Jesus?

You have read the evidence, or some of it.

Who do you say he is?

---

13   Mark 1:1, 11, 24; 3; 11; 9:7; 15:39.
14   Matthew 11:25–30; 16:16–18.

QUESTIONS FOR REFLECTION AND DISCUSSION:

1. Can you think of any other option that accounts for Jesus apart from those listed here?

2. What was the disciples' original attitude to Jesus and when and how did they change their attitude to him?

3. The New Testament has a view of who Jesus was and is. Where did that view originate?

FURTHER READING:

P.W. Barnett, *The Two Faces of Jesus* (Sydney, Hodder & Stoughton, 1990).

I.H. Marshall, *The Origins of Christology* (Leicester, IVP, 1977).

Chapter Ten

The claims of truth

The purpose of criminal court cases is that a jury can hear evidence and, on the basis of the evidence, reach a verdict about the accused.

The popular media regularly present the case against Jesus. The average person has heard many things about the supposed unreliability of the Bible and the flawed claims of Christ. Sensational new interpretations are routinely reported. Jesus was a magician. Jesus was a homosexual. The disciples were under the hallucinogenic influence of a sacred mushroom. Jesus escaped to Gaul and began a family from which an aristocratic French dynasty has come. Jesus was not crucified in Jerusalem but in Qumran, survived the ordeal, married several times and lived on until his seventies. Of Jesus' reported sayings only 18% are authentic. So on and on. These fantasies are reported in all seriousness by the media, with little if any opportunity to set the record straight.

Throughout this book the author has sought to present the evidence for Jesus – for his historical existence, his deity, his resurrection and for the historical reliability of the Gospels. In his opinion it is good evidence; in fact, outstanding evidence. Evidence from which a clear and conscientious verdict about Jesus can be reached.

Although a barrister is not at liberty to seek a 'not guilty' verdict where the client has told him he has committed the crime, doubt must sometimes remain in the advocate's mind. In arguing the truth claims of Jesus, this writer is utterly convinced about the case for Jesus. There is, in his opinion, no alternative but to accept the evidence as it stands. The ongoing procession of ingenious but improbable hypotheses about Jesus and alternative explanations to the resurrection only serve to show how rock-solid are the claims of Jesus as presented in the New Testament.

But the reader, like a jury member, must now come to a decision, reach a verdict about Jesus. For some, this may mean a serious re-think, a significant change of mind.

To illustrate, there was a time when I had my firm views about a celebrated murder case in Australia. In my opinion, the accused person – at that time in prison – was guilty. But a public meeting was held by those who believed there had been a miscarriage of justice. I went to the meeting, and heard a number of eyewitnesses of the alleged murder say that they were present at the time the murder was supposed to have occurred. Each in turn said that it would not have been possible for the accused to have committed the crime. On the basis of that eyewitness evidence, I changed my opinion, and in my own way, sought to persuade others about the strength of the evidence for the innocence of the accused. In time the miscarriage was recognised and the prisoner released. It was the evidence of the eyewitnesses that changed my mind.

Another illustration, from a different angle, may be seen in the case of the Holocaust where, it is claimed, millions of Jews were killed in detention camps during the 1930s and 1940s. Today there are some, mostly neo-fascists, who reject outright or radically modify the scale of the Holocaust. But the facts are there: the camps, the official records and above all the thousands of survivors who bear witness to the horrors of Hitler's 'final solution'. It is a case of ideological spectacles preventing the perception of facts and of truth. The Gospels express the eyewitness accounts of what the disciples saw Jesus do and heard Jesus say. Above all, they narrate his death and resurrection. But a sceptical ideology or cultural conditioning can blind one to the evidence for Jesus as it can also for the historicity of the Holocaust.

Two of the Gospel writers – Matthew and John – were eyewitnesses of Jesus. The other two – Mark and Luke – had close relationships with those who were eyewitnesses of Jesus. These four writers, who were in living contact with Jesus, give us evidence for the identity and resurrection of Jesus. It was because people saw Jesus with their own eyes and heard him with their own ears that they reached their conclusions.

You, the reader, are encouraged to accept the evidence of the Gospel writers and come to a conviction about Jesus, the Son of God, whom God raised from the dead. Like Peter, the centurion and Thomas, you are encouraged to express your conviction as confession to Jesus and about Jesus. You are encouraged to acknowledge Jesus Christ as Lord and to direct your trust in him for the forgiveness of your sins.

The evidence is there; you cannot simply turn your back on it. You are encouraged to accept the integrity of the evidence and confess that Jesus Christ is the Son of God.

But it does not stop there.

To accept the evidence about Jesus as the Son of God, risen from the dead, means adopting a 'position' about Jesus. This means, in turn, that you are conscientiously able to enter into a faith-commitment to the risen Christ as the Lord of your life, the One in whom you trust for the forgiveness of your sins.

But this now opens up a new and hitherto unimagined world. God's own Spirit comes to you, and imparts the sense that, like Jesus himself, you are the very child of God. His Father is now your Father. You enter the intimacy of trust with the almighty creator, the covenant God of Israel, in a deeply personal way. You approach God with the confidence of the child who comes to his parent asking for food or drink, knowing that he will not refuse you. It is, indeed, a 'new creation', as the apostle Paul said.[1]

---

1 2 Corinthians 5:17.

Submitting from the heart to Jesus as Lord means adopting his mind in all things, including his attitude to Scripture as the Word of God and as our final authority in all things relating to God and salvation.

To this point I have only asked you to accept the New Testament as authentically historical literature, which indeed it is. But this is a minimal position. As obedient from the heart to Jesus as Lord, you take a further step. The New Testament, along with the Old Testament, is Scripture; it is the breath of God, speaking to our hearts and minds.[2] The Scriptures inform us infallibly about who we are and who God is and how we can be reconciled to him through Jesus Christ. The 'new world' we have entered through Jesus is portrayed for us through the Bible as God's word to us. Our macro view of the world at large as well as our micro view of our personal world will now be informed and directed by God's self-revelation through the Scriptures.

It is sometimes said that the claims of Jesus are rejected, not because they have been examined and found wanting, but because they have been ignored. The reader has been presented with evidence for the truth about Jesus. Let that good evidence lead the reader to the only appropriate response: 'I believe'.

---

2   According to 2 Timothy 3:16 all scripture is 'God-breathed'.